D0480231

The Café Paradiso Cookbook

DENIS COTTER

PHOTOGRAPHS BY JÖRG KÖSTER

ATRIUM

First Published in 1999 by
ATRIUM,
Cork,
Ireland

3 5 7 9 10 8 6 4

Atrium is an imprint of Attic Press Ltd,
Crawford Business Park, Crosses Green, Cork.

Reprinted 2000, 2001, 2002

A CIP catalogue record for this book is available from the British Library.

ISBN 0 9535353 0 4 HB

Designed by John Foley at Bite! Associates, Cork
Additional photography by Paul Green
Scanning and separations by The Scanning Shop

Printed in China. Produced by Phoenix Offset.

Contents

Acknowledgements	vii
Introduction	1
Practical stuff	9
Wine	13
The pantry	15
Starters	43
Mains	89
Desserts	141
Index	165

". . . I now firmly believe that Cork's Café Paradiso is the only vegetarian restaurant – maybe in the whole of Europe – where the actual enjoyment of food is paramount. Like all recent converts to a cause I find myself seizing people by the arm and breathing unto them the name of the shrine, its location (Cork) and its Holy Book, *The Café Paradiso Cookbook.*"
Helen Lucy Burke

"Denis Cotter writes as he cooks, freely, cleverly, modestly, trusting to instinct and intuition. The result is a book without artifice or pretence, a book which rings utterly true."
John McKenna

"The spirit of Café Paradiso which I adore is captured in every page. I hugely admire their passion for fresh, naturally produced food and the creativity that Denis Cotter and his team bring to their menus. The mouth-watering prose alone is worth every penny."
Darina Allen

"This is a cookbook to treasure. If you love food, you will love this . . ."
Food and Wine

"Oh joy of joys – a beautifully produced, imaginative, unpretentious cookbook and – best of all – it's Irish!"
Image

"It's great to have a veggie cookbook that inspires you to drool over the recipes and cook them too!"
BBC Vegetarian Magazine

Café Paradiso
16 Lancaster Quay
Cork, Ireland
Tel +353 (0)21 277939
www.cafeparadiso.ie

Acknowledgements

IT ALMOST GOES BEYOND SAYING, but had better be said all the same, that boundless love and thanks go to Bridget Healy, my wife and partner in Café Paradiso, who would top most of the lists of acknowledgement below (except vegetable production!) and whose energy, taste and spirit define Café Paradiso more than anything or anyone else.

The production of this book, once I had written the recipes, was a much less stressful process than I had been led to expect. Certainly, I had the dream publishers in Atrium because I knew that they were almost as passionate about food as they were about books, a trait I noticed in just about everyone who worked on the book – not only was all of the food cooked for photography edible, but most of it was scoffed in the process. I want to give special thanks to the following: John Foley and Lisa Sheridan at Bite! Associates who took on the design work as a labour of love; Jörg Köster for his obsessive attention to detail with the photography; Eoin Kelly whose work on the cover is nothing like I imagined yet exactly what I hoped for; Mags Curtin for the dessert recipes; Marble & Lemon for allowing us to raid the shop; everyone in the Café Paradiso kitchen who kept the show on the road while my eye was off the ball, especially Jonathan, John and Mags. Also, Ger Cronin and Pat O'Brien for advice and testing.

The book is, of course, inseparable from Café Paradiso and I would like to take the opportunity to acknowledge the support of a number of people.

Those who made it possible for Bridget and I to open the doors – Mrs Mary Conroy for taking the risk of letting us into her building and being a brilliant landlady; my mother Mrs Kathleen Cotter for support whenever it was needed; David and Gretchen Healy; Jim O'Brien; Tanya, Mary and Jacinta; Ron Withington; Eoin Kelly and Leonie O'Dwyer; Michael and Brendan Cotter for design and printing.

And those who give it life now – the focused and dedicated cooks in the kitchen and the wizards in the dining room who make it into more than food, more than the sum of parts – Mags Curtin, Jonathan Leahy-Maharaj, John Healy, Sarah Hyland, Jean Kingston, Sandy Hyland, Tamzin Canniffe, Tara Vernon, Marie Cronin, Christine Moore, Jasmine O'Gorman, Triona Collins, Debbie Godsell, Rebecca Milne; the people who use the room for lunch, for dinner and as a café, the customers who take what we give in the spirit it is offered, who eat, drink, talk and laugh with pleasure and leave traces when they go.

The people who produce and supply the foods we work with, especially Organic Joe, Kim and Ian at Hollyhill and the Fresh Today boys for vegetables; Toby of the Real Olive Co.; Jenny Stokes for the best tofu I've ever come across; Munster Wholefoods; Wendy at Natural Foods; Sean, Josephine and Marian at Iago; Kevin Parsons and Joe Karwig for wines; Bill Hogan for Gabriel cheese; Wolfgang and Agnes at Knockalara; Fran at Forest Mushrooms; John and Mary at Mahers Coffee.

So many people have encouraged, supported and inspired me over the years, but I would like to acknowledge the influence of a few on my cooking: two American cooks and writers, Deborah Madison and Alice Waters, whose respectful approach to vegetables had a huge influence on food culture in general and helped me to change course; Nicola Wilde and Andrea du Chatenier in New Zealand whose gleeful but expert cooking was a joy to be around, and whose kitchen was a happy contradiction of the chefy notion that you need male aggression and tension to cook well; and Seamus O'Connell in Cork who encouraged me to cook from within myself, though he may not know it.

Denis Cotter

Introduction

It might seem like an obvious statement, but the food at Café Paradiso is produced mainly from vegetables, and a single vegetable is the foundation of almost every dish on our menus. Cheeses, oils, spices and herbs, breads and pastry, grains and nuts, are all brought along to enhance and play support to the vegetable in the starring role. From high summer to the end of the main harvest is the most wonderful time to be a vegetarian cook. Tomatoes, aubergines, sun-sweetened peppers, beans and peas – both familiar and strange – baby spinach, chard, soft herbs... The organic vegetable suppliers come to the restaurant laden with their pride and joy, freshly picked and bursting with the life-enhancing qualities that can't be measured in vitamin counts or calorie levels. A cook's job is to get the food to the customers with these qualities intact. But there are other high points in the year too, almost always centred on the arrival of the first batch of a favourite vegetable. Often it is just in time too, as the current favourite is on the wane and a vague sense of panic begins to creep in. Asparagus and new potatoes get huge cheers, of course, but so do pumpkins, black kale, leeks, beetroot, broad beans, artichokes and even parsnips. We can, it seems, get excited by the things other people push to the side of their plate. Every season has at least one hero and it is these vegetables that structure our year and dominate our menus during their high seasons. I say 'dominate' because of course not all our vegetables are organic or in high season all the time; in Ireland that would leave us eating stored roots and coarse cabbage during the 'hungry gap', that early spring period when we wait impatiently for the first fresh green things – spring greens, sprouting broccoli, asparagus – to grow.

And so our menus are by necessity filled out with the (now seemingly) seasonless peppers, aubergines and so on. Also it is becoming increasingly difficult, at least in the colder but wealthy northern European countries, to tell the seasons apart when our supermarkets are stocked with the same vegetables almost all year round. I believe it is crucial to recognise the hero of the season, the vegetables that are freshest and at their true prime, matured and ripened naturally in tune with the time of year, and then to offer them pride of place at the table and on my menus. It is hardly surprising that they almost always turn out to be organically grown as well, because the people who understand, in a holistic way, the nature of growing are inevitably committed to offering food that does more than look good. They grow organically, driven not only by the negative but worthy motive of avoiding chemicals, but in the positive knowledge that their way makes better food, food that not only tastes better but satisfies in a way that the eater can never quite put a finger on.

It was probably my involvement in vegetarian wholefood restaurants that left me with a deep commitment to working with organic foods. The core elements of these restaurants, that the ingredients we work with should be vegetarian and grown organically with care and respect, I brought with me when I set up Paradiso. A turning point in my thinking was when I read an article by a French woman against the increasing negativity of modern thinking on food which, she argued, could only result in the 'zero value' becoming the highest attribute of a dish, as in 'zero fat', 'zero sugar', 'zero taste' and so on. Vegetarianism is an ethic, not a diet, and that's all I'll say about that.

It was when Bridget and I went to live for a while in her native New Zealand that I first experienced seasonal eating as a physical reality rather than a fashionable concept. As we neared the end of the long, fascinating journey down the length of the North Island, we pulled over at a roadside stall where Gretchen bought two kilos of asparagus. We scoffed the lot for dinner as my London-learned food concepts did somersaults in my head. When the asparagus glut was over, there were new bounties to be exploited that continued through the summer until the high point of the sweetcorn pick-your-own frenzy. Bags of the stuff for a pittance, eaten within minutes or, at worst, hours of being picked. New Zealanders loved food in a way I had never encountered before. They loved to grow it, buy and sell it in vast piles of outrageously fine quality at insanely cheap prices, or so it seemed to me; and of course they loved to cook it with generosity and with a sense of freedom that seemed to come from the fact that they were throwing off their colonial culture and owed their allegiance, culinary or otherwise, to nobody. It is, I think, something that Ireland has in common with New Zealand. There are movements in Ireland to embrace the currently fashionable in food which is always good for a laugh and an expensive night out. There are movements to try to preserve our traditional food culture, which are worthy too, but there is so little there and what is there is a scrappy collection of dishes, some delicious but others

Paradiso
VICTORINOX
FUSION
BASA
house breads
gingered sweet potato spring roll on sesame greens
carrot, almond and feta terrine in vine leaves
penne in roasted garlic-parsley oil
fresh pasta in a lemon-thyme sauce
thai cashew & tofu sandwich fritters, pan-fried in a crisp corn coating
baked crepe of leeks, gabriel cheese & walnuts with a fennel sauce

only historically interesting, that hardly add up to a national culture. The opportunity that exists is, I believe, to accept that we have an almost blank page and to cook as we see fit from the finest produce we can muster. If that means cooking kale grown organically in West Cork in a style more familiar to Tibet, all the better. It will become our own culture much more than if we bought kale from Tibet and made colcannon of it. We must look to the growers first, encourage and reward them.

There is a story in one of the brilliant Tassajara cookbooks where Edward Espe Brown, a trained chef, tells of the day he decided it was ridiculous to go on pulling the spinach off its perfectly edible stalk, and how this simple thing opened up endless avenues for him as a cook.

I worked for a while in New Zealand with a couple of extraordinary women, Nick and Andrea, who ran and cooked in the Blues Café in Hamilton. They got up early every morning, did the muffin breakfast thing, trotted off a sparkling lunch, then sat down to concoct the evening dinner menu. Things got serious then. Maybe a raised voice or two, certainly a few quick parries and thrusts, then a mad dash to the shops and markets to pick up the necessary ingredients; come back and make adjustments for the stuff they couldn't get, then into the kitchen like a pair of tornadoes. They let me play along, offering me enough rope to do a couple of vegetarian dishes each evening. I learned to cook as best I could with the best ingredients available; and from the customers I learned to keep a rein on bizarre combinations, the bane of modern freestyle cooking. When an American couple passed through one evening and both ordered a dish I had never cooked before or have done since, then pronounced it better than anything they'd ever eaten in California, I swelled to twice my normal operational size for about an hour and a half of heady bliss, then drank far too much Thai whisky and fell asleep. I was honoured and knew how I wanted to cook. This relationship with the people who eat the food is an immeasurably important element in the development of my cooking and the spirit of Café Paradiso. Mind you, the floor staff all have such refined palates, fearless spirit and sharp tongues that if I only ever fed the staff I would have had to improve at least as much anyway.

This book is a collection of most of my favourite recipes from Café Paradiso that can be put down on paper with a degree of accuracy, though there are many recipes lost to time already and, I hope, many more out there yet beyond my understanding, as well as a few I really can't remember how to do. Through this collection of recipes I have tried to communicate how I cook and the wonderful things I cook with, more than cooking methods. I have travelled around the world a few times and stopped off briefly here and there, but I have only a limited knowledge of the various food cultures I have passed through. I do, however, have a magpie's eye for the shining bead and can recall, years later, what the air around a food stall in northern Thailand or southern Morocco smelled like, or the atmosphere in a Portuguese café where only the tomatoes and eggs were

vegetarian, but such tomatoes! Oh, and I have a large collection of ethnic cookbooks for train journeys and sleepless nights.

I have been told that I have a heavy hand – in general, that is, not just with seasoning but with just about everything. It's true, I admit it, every time I put in a generous handful, scoop or jugful, I toss in a little more just to be sure. To be simplistic about it, I believe that if you take the trouble to put a flavour into a dish, the person eating the dish might as well be able to taste it. It sounds moronically simple on paper but how often have you ordered food in a restaurant and been unable to remember what it was supposed to taste like according to the swaggering menu-speak? Two chillies in a pan, and a tablespoon of olive oil? I am very likely to put in another chilli along with a casual splash of the oil. How else will you know how far to go? Over the years I think I have learned to go to the edges of excess to concentrate flavours, yet appear almost refined, though I still get asked for a low-oil version of the pan-fried aubergine with the olive oil-rich sweet pepper concasse. To which I can only reply – of course, I'll give it a go. In a way, excess is the thing I add to the vegetables I cook with, as though to say 'you don't like kale, try this!' or 'see how strong that pumpkin – which you think so bland – really is, to stand its ground in this fiery company'. It is always to enhance the inherent character of the vegetable in question. My favourite way to cook, and the way that most of these recipes came about is to go stand in the tiny storeroom, pick out a vegetable to be hero for the night, then take it out into the bright lights of the kitchen. The other cooks usually stand behind me and, after a respectable period, yell 'carrots'. A bit of an in-joke that, I suppose. Over the years it's become much easier because of the relationships built up with growers and suppliers. Now I can do the standing in the storeroom bit in advance, and even in absentia, because I know the angels of West Cork will deliver the goods.

Some of the dishes in this book require a level of effort, skill and pre-planning that strains you a little, no matter how good a cook you are. I should hope so, they still stretch me and my fiercely efficient crew. No doubt you will also find some of the dishes to be what recipe books call 'supper dishes', things you can rattle off with your eyes half-closed and half a bottle of fine Sicilian wine on board. I find that the danger with simple food is that if it goes wrong there is no safety net below to save it from disaster, no mystery of the exotic, no near miss on that difficult technique to be applauded by those who otherwise think well of you. No, if a potato tortilla goes awry, or an omelette or toasted sandwich turn out dry and flavourless, then there is nowhere to turn and only your charm to live on. I love to work in that area where simple food done unbelievably well bowls people over, though I am old enough to accept that restaurant food needs to have airs of mystery and magic about it too.

Practical stuff

I know that people only very occasionally serve starters at home. Some of the starters here are very much just that – 'restaurant starters' and probably need to be saved for those rare occasions. Others, however, like the corn pancakes, the asparagus gratin or the spring rolls, are substantial or flexible enough to be served as a simple lunch or dinner, either by increasing the quantities or serving one or two other dishes with them. Similarly, the main courses range from simple pilaffs, risotto and pasta that can be knocked up in half an hour to more elaborate ones that probably need to be done in their entirety and at a relaxed pace.

The recipes in the pantry section are very often the things from which dishes are built, a collection of useful ways to cook various vegetables, grains, sauces, salsas and pestos. While most of the recipes were concocted for specific dishes on the restaurant menu, most of them have become part of our repertoire, our mental and actual larder, the kind of things you are very glad to find when you open the cupboard or the fridge, or to have at the back of your mind, before you know what to make for dinner. I think of these foods as my bag of tricks, things I put together in different ways to get various results. Adding even one new item to the bag can open up dozens of options. Now, I know it is a great luxury of a restaurant kitchen to be able to open a fridge to find an array of stimulating jars and bowls (and to have a couple of highly skilled people awaiting instructions), and I don't expect you to spend your every spare minute making polenta and a range of pestos, but if you become fond of even a few of these you will have expanded your own bag of tricks. Whether you use them in the way I do or divert them into your own style of cooking doesn't matter.

The desserts are practically all the work of Mags Curtin, our baking and pastry expert, who now has her own bench, a radio and almost-new fridge in the Paradiso kitchen. Some are perennials from the first menu, which I scraped together. I am half-ashamed to say that I am, in the matter of desserts, typical of most male Irish, and probably worldwide, cooks in paying only scant attention to the mysteries of 'afters'. I hope I am right in saying that Mags too loves to do the simple almost-familiar thing unbelievably well, and her desserts are a sublime, gentle, pleasure at the end of a meal. Most of the desserts included here were chosen to highlight a treatment of a specific fruit or two. As with vegetables, there are usually one or two fruits hitting their prime, especially from late spring to late autumn. When fruit is bursting with sunshine and sugar it needs very little embellishment. The recipes for organic strawberries or the gooseberry tart are perfect examples, though it could be argued that the best way to eat strawberries is by the huge bowlful with sugar and cream.

The quantities in the recipes are accurate where accuracy is important and in neat rounded figures when it is less so. As a cook, I am heavy-handed in that I use generous amounts of everything and then I put a little more in. This relates especially to the sources of rich flavour like olive oil, chillies, herbs, cheeses, coconut. I have done my best, in the recipes, to put in the 'generous' bit and leave out the 'little bit more'. All quantities are 'net', that is the amount going into the pot, not the amount brought home from the shop. For example, 500g of parsnips means 500g after peeling, and removing the cores if they are too woody.

Where eggs are used in a recipe, they are always medium size, though it doesn't often matter. Mind you, I've had more trouble from using too much egg, i.e. large ones, than too little.

Chilli quantities are a law unto themselves. We keep two types of chilli at all times and come across a few others during the course of the year. Our standard stock consists of fresh large red or green, and dried Thai 'bird's eye' – small, red and very hot. The dried ones we grind when we need them or keep a small jar of pre-ground, so the measurements can be in numbers of chillies or in teaspoonfuls. All measurements of dried chillies in the book are based on these little demons, so if you are using something milder or want a bigger or smaller hit, adjust accordingly. I have tried to give an indication of whether a dish with chillies is to be dominated by it, moderately hot or if the chilli is only a seasoning. I think the best thing is to use one type of chilli regularly and get to know its strength. This might also be true of fresh chillies, but in practice it is impossible to predict. A friend of mine who grows chillies says you can get wildly varying strengths even from the same bush. The only thing to do is taste them. Using the seeds to vary the strength is a good idea. If the flesh is very mild, leave in some or all of the seeds; if it is hot, well, at least you know what you're dealing with. Good luck.

We seem to have a huge range of oils in the kitchen at any one time. Some are used in small quantities for flavouring only, such as hazelnut, almond and walnut, truffle, toasted sesame oil, though we get through quite a bit of the sesame because I love what it does for fried vegetables, noodles and salads. For general light frying and for salads in which the flavour of the oil is not meant to be a presence, we use sunflower, soya or rapeseed – there is little difference. For deep-frying, we use corn or peanut oil. That leaves the olive oils, of which we seem to go through a small lake's worth every week. We keep three on hand at all times. A light, cheaper one to use when cooking, for

example when frying the couscous-crusted aubergine on page 126, in a heated concasse or when wilting greens as on page 20. A good quality extra virgin oil whenever the oil is used raw or only slightly warmed – for salad dressings, pesto, cold sauces such as the harissa-sweet pepper oil, salsas, with pasta or risotto, indeed anywhere where the flavour of the oil might add to the dish. Finally, we keep a special oil to offer customers as a dip for bread, something with a big, fruity and spicy flavour – at the moment this is an organic Portuguese oil. I know some people feel we use a lot of oils and fats in our cooking and this may come through in these recipes. My feeling is that when you start with intrinsically low-fat produce, as vegetables are, then there's a lot more scope to add a drop or two more along the way. If you're worried, take the advice of a famous Irish restaurant critic who answered charges of gluttony by claiming that she only ate porridge the next day. A last word on the subject of oils and fats; when a recipe calls for butter it means butter. I can't really see the point of butter substitutes, except for vegans whose need for them is at least based on a strongly felt ethic.

Cheeses, when used in cooking, almost fall into the same category as oils, given that we use them to add richness and intense flavours to vegetable dishes that would be too light or one-dimensional without them. Some cheeses seem to have an affinity for certain vegetables, such as goat's cheese with leeks or aubergines, feta with spinach and onions, Parmesan with rocket, tomatoes or peppers, and my favourite – asparagus with Gabriel, a Swiss-style thermophilic cheese from West Cork made by Bill Hogan in physically impressive five or six kilo rounds. Over the last twenty years, the range of Irish-made cheeses, and particularly Cork-made cheeses, has expanded exponentially. The cheeses, though based on classic styles, often wear the name of their locality as this influences their character as much as location does a wine's character. For me, the brilliant thing about this development is the high quality of the cheeses, something which surely comes from the fact that the producers seem to make the cheese primarily from a love of, and lust for, their favourite cheese. In Café Paradiso, we use cheese mainly for cooking and salads, and a small collection of favourites that work well in our cooking style appear again and again, along with well known european cheeses like Parmesan, feta, goats milk chevre-style, Stilton and mozzarella. In fact, one or two of my own favourite cheeses hardly ever make an appearance in the restaurant; I'm thinking especially of Coolea, a gouda-style cheese from Coolea (!) near Macroom in Mid-Cork which manages, when mature, to be both sublime and stunning at the same time. This highlights a problem when buying cheese. Very often, especially in supermarkets or where cheeses are pre-cut and plastic-wrapped, this is done when the cheese has not yet ripened and so never does, leaving the customer wondering what all the fuss was about. This is why it is best to buy cheese from a shop that cuts from the block each time and where the sellers know their cheese and who buy and store well, so that they are always selling the cheeses at an optimum stage of maturity. I tip my hat to the makers of the following cheeses which feature regularly in our cooking:

Ardsallagh, a fresh, mild goat's milk cheese from east Cork; Knockalara, a similar fresh style but from sheep's milk in Cappoquin in Waterford; the aforementioned Gabriel from Schull in West Cork, a hard, aged cheese with lingering peppery, sharp flavours; Gubeen from West Cork, a semi-hard cheese – we use the lightly smoked version which is, I think, one of the few justifications for smoking food I've come across; Ardrahan from North Cork; St. Brendan brie; and Cooleeney goat's milk brie.

MEASUREMENTS USED IN THE RECIPES

dstspn = dessert spoon

tblspn = table spoon

tsp = tea spoon

TEMPERATURE CONVERSIONS USED IN THE RECIPES

°C	°F	Gas Mark
110	225	¼
120	250	½
140	275	1
150	300	2
160	325	3
180	350	4
190	375	5
200	400	6
220	425	7
230	450	8
240	475	9

Wine

The wine list in Café Paradiso has grown over the years from an initial stock of twelve popular bottles to around fifty carefully chosen wines, and is constantly evolving. The reason for this is simple: we love to buy wine, we love to drink wine, we even like to sell it, and an encouraging number of our customers seem to like drinking it too. Because the food menus are vegetarian as well as eclectic, the wine list has taken shape gradually from a combination of our personal tastes and a need to accumulate wines that will complement the wide range of tastes in the food. The wine list is, of course, all the more idiosyncratic due to Bridget's total ban on french wines since the bombing of the Greenpeace Rainbow Warrior ship in Auckland Harbour in 1985, a gesture which she enjoys all the more when wine-francophiles see it as single-issue and provocative. Wines are added to the list, and dropped, through an ongoing very personal process of reading, tasting and talking involving Bridget, Sarah and Jean, our suppliers Kevin Parsons and Joe Karwig and some very dedicated customers. I like the organic nature of this: we help people to choose what they will drink of an evening, and their feedback helps us to build and maintain our wine list.

It seems to me that most people, when deciding what to eat and drink, keep the notion of matching food and wine in their minds, but towards the back. Quite often they simply choose their favourite wine and their favourite food dishes. Certainly, giving some thought to which wine you drink with a dish can add to the pleasure of a meal, but only if you actually like to drink that wine in the first place. There is no point in insisting that someone drink, say, a delicate white italian wine with their tempura if they have come in the door fantasising about their favourite Californian cabernet.

The underlying guidelines for matching wine to food are, I think, essentially the same for vegetarian food as other dishes. Wine and food are best when equals are pitted together, when the two are complementary and allow each other's character to shine through. Common sense therefore suggests that subtle foods need subtly flavoured wines and that dishes with lots of strong flavours, rich oily textures, smelly cheeses and the like, will need a formidable companion. Trying to balance opposites will always result in one or other being overpowered. Rich foods need big, full-flavoured wines to stand up to them and the wines in turn need the fat and proteins of rich food to counter the tannins. Asian-spiced foods present a unique challenge, dishes which are usually dominated by big flavours, spices such as ginger, chillies, coriander etc. but are light in texture, low in fats and certainly not rich or heavy foods. Some specific grape varieties have been found, by trial and error, to be perfect partners for these dishes, especially Gewürztraminer, Riesling, Malvasia and some New Zealand sauvignon blancs, the ones bursting with tropical fruit flavours.

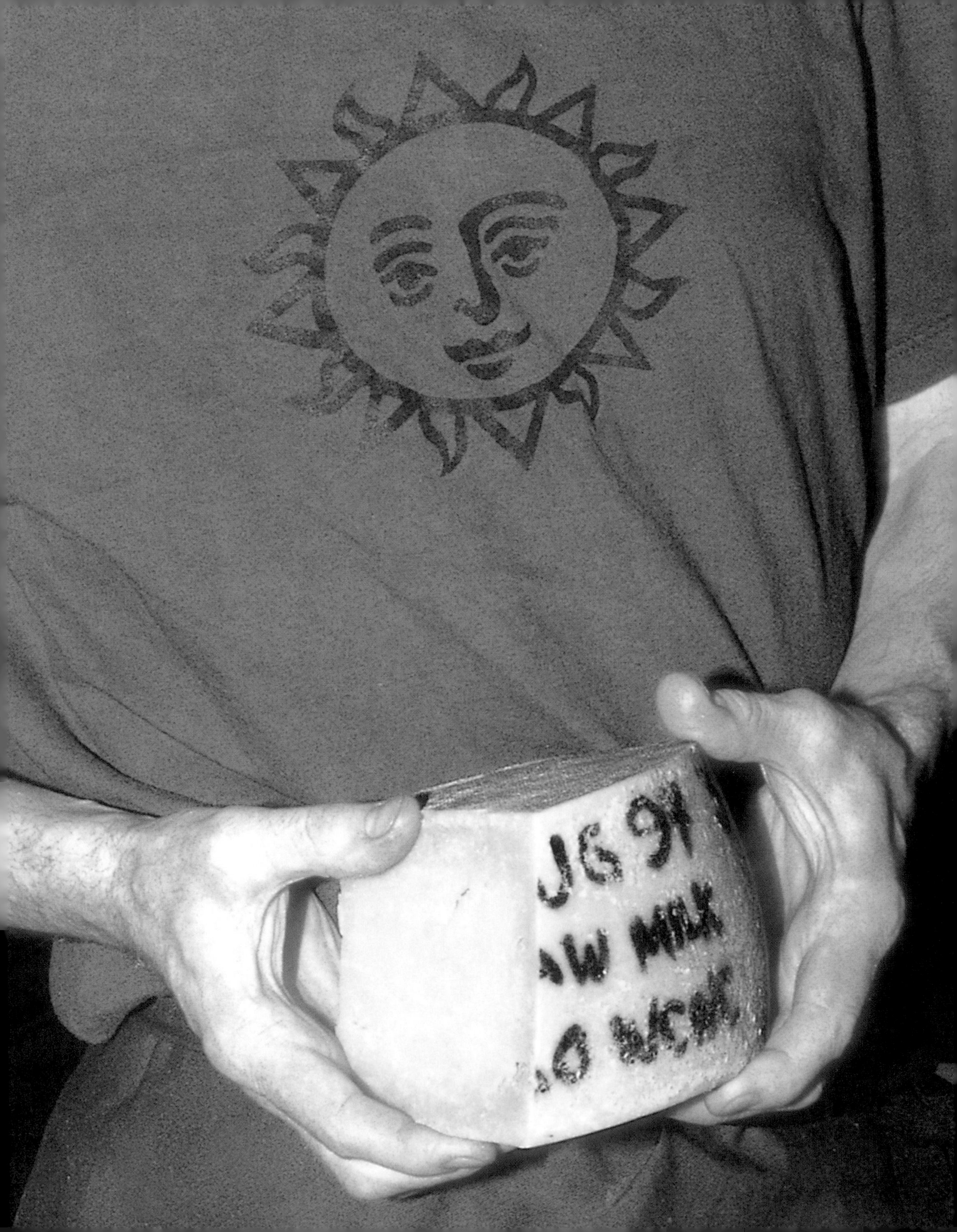

The pantry

Rosemary, tomato and onion bread ¶ Focaccia sandwich ¶ Grilled aubergine ¶ Roasted peppers ¶ Green beans with garlic and lemon ¶ Wilted greens ¶ Balsamic-roasted beetroot ¶ Wasabi mash ¶ Leek and smoked cheese mash ¶ Braised fennel ¶ Braised puy lentils ¶ Spiced roast potatoes ¶ Ginger-roasted sweet potatoes ¶ Chilli-roasted squash ¶ Chickpeas with chillies ¶ Sesame-fried cabbage ¶ Fragrant basmati rice ¶ Lemon-buttered couscous ¶ Felafel ¶ Green pepper-coriander salsa ¶ Fennel-chilli salsa ¶ Avocado salsa ¶ Harissa-sweet pepper oil ¶ Pineapple chutney ¶ Chermoula ¶ Black olive tapenade ¶ Pesto ¶ Basil pesto ¶ Rocket pesto ¶ Coriander-chilli pesto ¶ Sundried tomato pesto ¶ Basil oil, rosemary-chilli oil and coriander-lime oil ¶ Aioli from herb oils ¶ Polenta

Rosemary, tomato and onion bread

Bread is the basis of it all, the staple food of most of Europe and beyond. Bread wakes up our kitchen early in the morning, and comes to life as the kitchen does, finally emerging from the oven when the place has become a flurry of activity, smells, noise and a slight nervousness about the impending lunch. I can't imagine working in a restaurant kitchen that didn't make its own bread.

At Paradiso we make five different breads every day, if you don't count the bagels which I'm proud to say (while cunningly withholding the recipe) are as good a bagel as you'll get on this side of the Atlantic . The breads are all cut from the same cloth, as it were, so I'm giving you my own favourite here. It's a soft bread, rich in olive oil and rosemary. To adapt the recipe, simply replace the rosemary with whatever you fancy, but don't put anything on top except olive oil. Chopped olives or some leftover tapenade or pesto make a great bread, sliced walnuts and chives are good, and we often simply add loads of chopped herbs and bake the dough in a loaf tin. Don't get carried away though; it is possible to spoil the primal pleasure of bread with fancy-dan tactics. We use an organic, stoneground, strong white flour from Doves Farm in England, widely available in Ireland also. There is only one good reason for doing this, and it's not our health, our bowels or our image. No, it simply has a great flavour. When so much refined white flour is tasteless powder and almost all of Europe's white sticks of bread come from central production units, it is essential to use a good flour to make your bread and people love bread that has its own honest flavour.

This recipe makes two flatbreads of 650g each. Make only one if you like (though it's hard to work such a tiny dough), or make the dough into one larger, slightly higher loaf, as long, wide and high as your oven will take. The finished loaves freeze well, and you'll be glad to have one to warm up when you get back from the beach late on a Sunday.

FOR TWO FLATBREADS OF 650g EACH:

- 3 tsps dried active yeast
- 2 scant tsps sugar
- 800g strong flour
- 400mls warm water
- 2 tsps salt
- 2–3 sprigs fresh rosemary, leaves only
- 100mls olive oil
- 1 onion, sliced in thin half-rounds
- 4 tomatoes, thinly sliced and deseeded

MIX THE YEAST, sugar and 300g of the flour in a large bowl, then stir in the warm water. Somewhere in the region of body temperature is the ideal warmth of the water: test by sticking your finger in it for a few seconds. Leave this to get on with its business for three or four minutes but no more – the yeast will become activated and cause the mix to puff up a little and become spongy. If nothing happens, chuck it all out and try again. Now add in the rest of the flour, the salt, rosemary and olive oil. Use first a wooden spoon to bring it all together, then your hands to finish the gathering up and to tip it out on to the worktop. Begin kneading in your own inimitable style, to your favourite kneading music, and keep doing it until you lose interest or ten minutes passes, whichever is longer. (Three standard pop tunes or one meandering jazz odyssey is just about right.) Brush the inside of the bowl with olive oil, put the dough in, creased side down, brush the top of the dough and leave it in a warm, not hot, place for about 30 minutes or until the dough has about doubled in size. When it has, punch it down, or gently push it if you're sensitive, and cut the dough in two with a sharp knife. On a lightly floured worktop, roll one of the pieces to a thickness of about 15mm in a roughly rectangular shape. It should sit in a 26 x 36 Swiss-roll tray, though it doesn't have to. The dough is a very manageable and elastic one, though you should still be

careful not to stretch or tear it. Set the dough on a parchment-lined flat oven tray, or that Swiss-roll tray, brush the top with olive oil and scatter the onion slices on it. Next, arrange the tomato slices on top and press them down gently. Set the dough in a warm place to rise again and repeat with the second piece of dough. They will take another 20 minutes or so to rise again to nearly double their thickness. Use this time to set the oven to the right temperature, 350°F (Gas Mark 4), and to clean up the mess you made. Bake the loaves for 12–15 minutes, turning them on the horizontal once if they need it. A conventional oven will give the loaves a soft, pale finish, while a fan-assisted oven will cook them faster, browner and with crisper crusts. Both ways are fine; you're lucky if you have the choice.

Focaccia sandwich

with roasted vegetables, tapenade and goats' cheese

A recipe to turn one of the bread loaves into a meal. Though I've given specific vegetables and a cheese here, what I would really recommend is that you use what you've got and like. For me, the fennel is vital in the mix, but if you don't like fennel don't use it.

- 1 medium aubergine
- olive oil
- 1 red onion
- ½ fennel bulb
- 1 small red or yellow pepper
- 1 medium courgette
- 8 cloves garlic, halved
- 1 rosemary, tomato and onion loaf (see page 16)
- 3 tblsps tapenade (see page 35)
- fresh herbs: any of basil, parsley, oregano, marjoram
- 150g goats' cheese, sliced

SLICE THE AUBERGINE crossways into rounds about 10mm thick, cut these in half, brush them with oil and roast them in a hot oven, 380–400°F (Gas Mark 5–6), for ten to twelve minutes until cooked through and browned. Meanwhile slice the red onion and fennel in thin quarter-rings, toss them in olive oil in an oven dish and put them into the hot oven while you chop the other vegetables. Quarter the pepper, then slice these pieces across, not too thin, then slice the courgette similarly into fat matchsticks. Add these vegetables and the garlic to the onion and fennel, add a little more oil and return them to the oven until they are tender and browning. Check them often and stir them around now and then. It should take 15 minutes or so. Then turn the oven down to 350°F (Gas Mark 4).

Carefully slice the bread in half horizontally, and spread the tapenade on the bottom piece, then cover that with a layer of the aubergines. Season the other vegetables and spread them over the aubergine slices. Next scatter on any fresh herbs you're using, then place a layer of cheese slices. Put the top piece of the loaf back on and press lightly on it. Wrap the loaf, or sandwich as it may now be called, in foil and put it back in the oven. It's a bit messy to be regularly checking something wrapped in foil, so leave it for 20 minutes before you have a look. It will be done then or in another ten. The cheese will be melting and the whole thing warmed through. If you like a more 'baked' effect, take the foil off for the last five minutes of cooking; if you want a more all-melded-into-one finish, cook the wrapped sandwich at a lower temperature for longer. I've done loaves three times this size very low for two hours, with brilliant results.

Leave the sandwich to rest for a few minutes when it comes out of the oven, then cut it into as many pieces are there are people sitting at your table. With a salad of lettuce leaves and any other greens with olive oil and balsamic vinegar this will make a fine lunch. If you can, eat it outside with a bottle of something light and crisp.

Grilled aubergine

A raw aubergine, though handsome and exotic, is about as inedible and unappetising a vegetable as you could sink your teeth into. Even at that, it's a bit fussy about how it's cooked. I've never eaten boiled aubergine and it doesn't appeal to me, and because it absorbs so much oil when fried, grilled or roasted it is important to use a good olive oil, as that will be an essential part of the cooked flavour. Any of these cooking methods will turn an aubergine into one of the most flavoursome, adaptable and useful vegetables.

Very often the first thing I do to start an aubergine dish is to slice it and then grill the slices. The result is one of the most useful things in a vegetarian cook's armoury. It isn't only for the rich, intense, roasted flavour that I cook aubergine this way, but also because it is so easy to control the degree of cooking, the texture, shape and size of the aubergine slices. Strictly speaking, the way we do it is more roasted than grilled. A good fan oven with even, dry heat is perfect, otherwise use a grill. The method is simply this: cut the aubergine into slices of the size, thickness and shape you want, brush the slices on both sides with a good olive oil, place them on an oven tray and roast them at 350–400°F (Gas Mark 4–6) for about ten minutes, until the aubergine is cooked through. Remember that aubergine shrinks a bit when cooked and do please cook it soft; undercooked aubergine is disgusting. A perfectly grilled or roasted aubergine slice is lightly browned on the outside but yields meltingly on the inside. The time and temperature depend to an extent on the thickness of the slices. I think thicker slices cook better if given a little more time at a slightly lower temperature. For grilling, place the oiled slices under a hot grill until browned and cooked, turning them once. Chargrilling, though very fashionable spasmodically, is for addicts only – the char or smoky flavour almost always outweighs that of the vegetable and usually the process leaves the vegetable revoltingly raw inside or completely burned.

Once you've got into the habit of cooking aubergines this way, there are millions of uses for it. For pasta dishes, do thinnish round slices, then halve them and add them to the pasta sauce. Lengthways slices can be rolled around a stuffing, layered into a bake or a sandwich like the recipe for aubergine gamelastra on page 133. In fact there are loads of recipes scattered through the book which are based on grilled aubergines.

Roasted peppers

As with aubergines, roasted peppers are an excellent part of an antipasti, but the roasting and peeling of peppers is usually a preliminary step in many pepper dishes. The basic technique is this: place the peppers under a hot grill or over a flame, and turn them occasionally until their skins are loosened and partly blackened. Pop the peppers into a plastic or paper bag or a bowl covered with clingfilm, and leave them to cool – ten minutes should do it but longer will be kinder to your hands. Now peel off the skin and lose the seeds. The roasting can also be done in an oven, but the pepper flesh will cook more than under a grill, which may not be suitable for some dishes. Either way, you now have peeled roasted peppers to be turned into stuffing wrappers, sauces, oils, pastes, soups, anything you fancy.

Green beans with garlic and lemon

I first did these as a side dish to add a fresh and sharp element to a rich, spicy Moroccan-style meal. It's a lovely way to present very fresh beans at their best and a bowlful on the table will happily go with almost any meal. They are served at room temperature, by the way, which makes them equally good as part of a salad or antipasti starter.

FOR SIX:

- 300g green beans
- 4 cloves of garlic
- 100ml olive oil
- salt and pepper
- rind and juice of ½ lemon

TOP AND TAIL THE BEANS, then cook them in boiling water for a few minutes until just tender. Cool them in cold water immediately. Thinly slice the garlic cloves and put them in a small pan with the olive oil. Heat this very gently for a few minutes to soften the garlic a little – just to take the raw sharpness from it. Try not to boil the oil, it won't do any good at all. Leave the oil to cool almost to room temperature before pouring it and the garlic over the beans. Season with salt and pepper. This can be done up to a few hours before serving, but add the lemon just before serving – it can discolour the beans if they are left sitting in it for too long. Also, don't add all the lemon at first, try a little and taste it.

Wilted greens

A mound of greens, briefly wilted over high heat, is a great foil for any kind of rich food, even though it has a little olive oil in it too. I use this a lot, sometimes unnamed mixes of miscellaneous greens, sometimes one specific variety. Spinach, though not delicate young 'real' spinach, and chard are excellent; kale is coarser but is my favourite, especially the black Italian variety which cooks to such a dark, vivid green. Small amounts of other greens like rocket, beet leaves and frisée and the like add a complexity to the flavours if you're using a mix. These don't all cook at the same rate, so either start with the coarsest leaves and add the others according to their delicacy, or toss them all in together, compromise on the cooking time and take delight in the textural differences you end up with. The quantities for greens are difficult to measure, so I would suggest you need a large handful for each person.

FOR FOUR:

- 4 large handfuls of greens
- olive oil
- 1 red onion, thinly sliced
- salt and black pepper

TEAR THE LEAVES INTO PIECES – kale needs to be in smaller pieces than, say, spinach. If the greens need to be washed, shake them but leave some water clinging to them. Heat about two tablespoons of olive oil to a high temperature in a large pan. Put in the red onion, stirring constantly for half a minute, then put in all the greens and keep stirring them over a high heat. An occasional splash of water will help the process and ensure that the greens are wilting and not frying, but only tiny amounts of water at a time. The greens are done when they have completely changed colour to a darker green, softened and shrunk – this should only take about a minute for spinach and chard, maybe two for kale. Turn the heat off, season well with salt and pepper, and get the greens out of the pan quickly. It's better to eat them at room temperature than to overcook them.

Balsamic-roasted beetroot

A splash of balsamic vinegar gives an interesting twist to roasted beetroot, which on its own can become almost too sweet to qualify as savoury food.

FOR FOUR:

- 6–8 small beetroots
- olive oil
- 1 tsp balsamic vinegar

BOIL THE BEETROOTS without trimming them or cutting them in any way. This will help to preserve their extraordinary colour. How long a beetroot takes to cook will depend, among other things, on its size and how long it's been stored since taken out of the ground; it can be from 20 minutes to an hour-and-a-half or more. After 20 minutes, gingerly pierce one with a fork or a sharp knife to test for tenderness. A beetroot will never cook to soft, but it will change from unyielding rawness to a cooked tenderness. Drain the beetroots and put them, pot and all, in the sink. Cover the roots with cold water and, with the cold water running over them, use your fingers to rub off the skin. If the skin doesn't come off easily, the roots are probably aged, gnarled old things and the only remedy is to take a peeling knife to them. The roots are now ready to be eaten or subjected to a second stage of cooking.

For balsamic-roasted beetroot, slice the small roots in half (bigger ones should be sliced into four or six orange-segment type pieces), put them on an oven tray, brush them with just enough olive oil to coat them and roast them in a moderate-hot oven (325–400°F, Gas Mark 3–6) until the roots are crisping and caramelizing at the edges. Turn them once or twice to get an even finish. Towards the end of the cooking, as the roots caramelize, pour in the balsamic vinegar and toss the roots in it. Cook for five minutes more.

カネク®
粉わさび
高級品
BRAND Wasabi

Wasabi mash

Wasabi works brilliantly in mash, better than European mustards, I think. I love the way its pungency strikes, threatens to blow your head off, then disappears just as panic is about to set in. The texture and richness of mash contain and cushion the effect, though not enough to take the fun out of it. How much to use is one of those personal things that only trial and error will solve for you, but the quantities below should cause a little drama. The instruction 'stir wasabi into mashed potato' is all that's required here if you're a happy potato masher. But if you weren't paying attention when your mother was trying to teach you, or you lost the knack during its years of being unfashionable, this will help. The quantities of everything, as ever, depend on the degree of flouriness of the potatoes. Someone should invent a scale of flouriness to be marked on potatoes for sale. In Ireland almost all the common varieties for sale are floury and perfect for mashing and roasting – Records, Kerr's Pink, Golden Wonders, British Queens. Roosters, which are becoming more common here, are a kind of halfway house to waxy varieties and not so good for mashing, though still fine for roasting. Warming the milk and butter helps to stretch the starch of the potatoes, giving a fluffier mash. An energetic mashing arm is crucial too.

FOR FOUR:

- 800g floury potatoes
- 60g butter
- 150–200mls milk
- salt and pepper
- 2 tsps wasabi powder

PUT THE POTATOES IN A POT of cold water, bring to the boil and cook at a rolling boil until the potatoes are cooked through. Peel the potatoes while they are still hot and put them back in the pot over a low heat for a couple of minutes to dry them. The drier the potatoes, the fluffier your mash will be. At the same time, warm the butter and milk together until the butter is just melting. Then use a potato masher to mash the potatoes thoroughly with the butter and milk. Season well with salt and a little pepper before adding the wasabi – use white pepper if you don't want your mash flecked with black dots. Make a paste with the wasabi powder and a little water or milk, then stir it into the mash. Taste, then add more wasabi if you need to.

Leek and smoked cheese mash

Generally, I don't like smoked foods. It's one of those flavours, like chargrilling, that people become addicted to, to the extent that it doesn't matter what's been smoked or charred. I've had chargrilled aubergines served to me that might as well have been scorched shoe insoles. I use smoked Gubeen cheese, which is so delicately smoked that the process actually seems to add something to the cheese. If you use another cheese, you might want to reduce the quantity. The effect you want in this dish is flecks of barely cooked leek and melting pockets of cheese scattered through the mash.

FOR FOUR:

- 800g floury potatoes
- 60g butter
- 150mls milk
- salt and pepper
- 1 leek, finely chopped
- 2 cloves of garlic, finely chopped
- 100g mild smoked cheese, in small dice

MASH THE POTATOES according to the recipe for wasabi mash, or in your own unbeatable way. While the potatoes are cooking, slice the leeks in half lengthways almost to the base and wash them carefully under running water. Chop the leek finely and fry it with the garlic in a third of the butter for a few minutes, until the leek is beginning to soften but retaining its colour. Just before you serve the mash, stir in the leek and the smoked cheese. It's best if the cheese only partly melts.

Braised fennel

Any method of cooking fennel that doesn't throw away the flavour with the water is good but this is one of the best, I think. To cook fennel with pasta I always stew slices of it in olive oil or butter first and toss the lot into the pasta dish. Fennel is excellent also in a stock base because it leaks its flavour so easily into water. It is really important that you get fennel bulbs that are very firm, white and preferably fat - endlessly removing expensive, stringy layers can be very depressing. As an accompaniment, you will need from half to one bulb per person, depending on size.

FOR FOUR:

- 2–4 fennel bulbs
- 2 tblspns olive oil
- 75mls white wine
- 75mls water

TRIM A BIT OFF THE END of the fennel bulb, then cut it lengthways into four or six pieces. You may have to lose the outer layer if it seems stringy or tough. Heat two tablespoons of olive oil in a heavy pan and toss the fennel in it. Cook at a moderate heat for five minutes or so, then pour in half a glass of white wine, the same of water and some seasoning. Bring to the boil, cover and simmer for five minutes. Now transfer the lot to a warmed oven dish and cover with foil (or better still put the pot in the oven if it is that kind of pot). Cook for 15 minutes in a moderate oven, turn the fennel and continue cooking until the fennel is tender and lightly browned in places – another 15 minutes should do it but that depends on the fennel and the oven. If you're not in a hurry, slow and gentle is best.

Braised puy lentils

Put 'vegetarian' and 'lentil' together in a sentence these days and you find everybody making their excuses and leaving. I think I've probably already eaten my lifetime's share of lentils, which might explain why we use them so sparingly in Café Paradiso. I love red lentils in thick spiced soups in the winter, and dhals of course, especially with coconut. And then there's this recipe, variations on which are the basis of how we almost always prepare puy lentils. I don't know if it is technically correct to call this braising; because we are making it up as we go in Paradiso, we seem to have evolved a vocabulary of redefined and nearly-correct usages of catering terms. Anyway, this is a great way to add to the flavour and richness of lentils without drowning out their own character. Jonathan, a Café Paradiso cook, calls it speed-braising, and that's as good a description as I've heard. The finished dish can act as a grounding, earthy element in the balancing of all kinds of rich meals, especially with aubergines and salty cheeses like goats', blue or feta.

FOR SIX:

- 120g puy lentils
- 1 tomato, deseeded and diced
- 1 small red onion, finely chopped
- small handful fresh parsley or basil
- 50mls olive oil
- salt and pepper

PUT THE LENTILS IN A POT of cold water, bring it to the boil and simmer until the lentils are just tender or a fraction short of it, then drain them and return them to the pot with the tomato, red onion and herbs. Pour in the olive oil and 100mls water, bring it to the boil and cook at a lively simmer until the water has evaporated and the lentils are coated in the gloss of the olive oil. This should take five minutes or thereabouts and the tomato and onion should have softened a little. If you want them softer, simply add more water and boil vigorously for a few minutes more. Season generously with salt and pepper.

Spiced roast potatoes

At home we cook potatoes this way when we feel like it, irrespective of the main dish they are supposedly accompanying. You know those evenings when the meal is built around the potatoes you crave. The combination of spices varies as does the intensity of the heat of chillies or pepper, so this recipe is only a sample of endless variations. The basic technique is useful, if you don't know it. The ideal potato for this is a small round floury one, though bigger ones cut into two-bite chunks are fine.

FOR FOUR:

- 800g potatoes, peeled
- 2 small dried chillies
- 1 tsp cumin seeds
- 1 tsp black peppercorns
- ½ tsp salt
- 2 tblspns butter
- 3 tblspns olive oil

CHOP THE POTATOES into two-bite chunks if you can't find any small enough to do whole. Put them in a pot, cover with cold water and bring to the boil. Simmer (covered), for about 5 minutes to soften the outsides, then drain the potatoes and return them to the pot. Put it over a low heat for a minute or two to dry the potatoes. Now, put the lid on the pot tightly and shake the pot vigorously a few times to bash the potatoes off the inside of the pot and each other. This will give them lovely fluffy, battered edges. Perfect for holding the spices and absorbing the butter and oil. Meanwhile, use a spice grinder or a mortar and pestle to chop the chilli, cumin and pepper into a coarse grind and add the salt. Heat the oven to about 400°F (Gas Mark 6). Put the butter, spices and a tablespoon of olive oil in a roasting dish and put the dish in the oven for a few minutes to melt the butter. Put the potatoes in the dish, tossing them well to coat them fairly evenly with the spices. Roast the potatoes until the edges are crisped and the insides well done, about 40 minutes.

Ginger-roasted sweet potatoes

This is essentially the same as the recipe for chilli-roasted squash (opposite), using ginger instead of chilli. The sweet potatoes behave very like the squash, so obviously these recipes are interchangeable, the ginger version being a good foil for hot-spiced dishes. Use either the yellow-fleshed sweet potatoes or the paler, pink-skinned ones which are not as sweet but still have that melting texture. If you don't mind a little cheating, a teaspoon of honey melted with the butter will do wonders for unsweet sweet potatoes.

FOR FOUR:

- 4–6 sweet potatoes, about 500g
- 2 tblspns butter
- 1 tblspn grated ginger
- ¼ salt

PREHEAT THE OVEN to 380°F (Gas Mark 5), though anything from 320–420°F (Gas Mark 3–7) will be okay if the potatoes have to share the oven. Peel the sweet potatoes and cut them into rounds of about 15mm thick. Put the butter in an oven dish with a little cooking oil and melt it in the oven for a minute. Toss the potato chunks with the ginger and a little salt in the butter, then roast them until soft and browned. They will need to be turned once or twice during the cooking.

Chilli-roasted squash

There are a few recipes throughout the book featuring squashes and pumpkins in various guises. The most common way for them to show up on a Paradiso menu, however, is treated fairly simply and used as a secondary part of a dish or on the side. This is true at home too, and in New Zealand where I first made their acquaintance. There, many dinners were accompanied by huge wedges of pumpkin (Crowns, usually), slowly roasted until meltingly soft and eaten with butter, skins and all. A lovely way to cook a whole, smallish squash is to slice off the top, scoop out the seeds, put in some garlic butter, replace the top and bake in a moderate oven until a knife goes easily through the flesh. We sometimes get a few tiny 'Jack-be-littles' which are brilliant like this, one per person. I love chilli with squash, especially if there's some butter involved too. It's got all the comforting, melt-in-the-mouth qualities but with an added touch of excitement. I'd eat this for breakfast but what it's perfectly suited to is accompanying dishes flavoured with interesting but mild flavours. The skin of most squashes and pumpkins is edible but that's up to you. This recipe is simple and works equally well on any kind of squash or pumpkin, but is best with the orange-fleshed sweet varieties. The quantities are all dependent on the size of the pumpkin. Three of the wedges described below will be a substantial amount for each person. If your squash is bigger than that, cook only as much as you want and the leftover piece will keep for a day or two, or longer if wrapped in paper and kept in the fridge.

FOR SIX:

- 1 small pumpkin or squash, about 1–1.5kg
- 30g butter
- 4 dried 'bird's-eye' chillies or equivalent
- ¼ tsp salt

The worst part of dealing with pumpkins, especially large hard-skinned ones, is cutting them down to manageable pieces without injury. Be careful. First chop the squash in half and scoop out all the seeds and stringy stuff. Now place the halves cut-side down on a board and carefully chop them into smaller pieces until you have wedges of about two- or three-bite size. Toss these in just enough butter to coat them, enough chopped chilli to tickle your palate and some salt. You can speed up the process by boiling the wedges in water for a minute first, but they cook very quickly in water and will fall apart in the oven if they have been cooked too much already. Roast the wedges in a fairly hot oven, 350–400°F (Gas Mark 4–6), until the squash is soft and caramelizing at the edges, tossing and turning them once or twice in the process. About 20 minutes should do it.

Chickpeas with chillies

The chilli-heat rating of this dish depends on the chillies you use and your own tolerance for the stuff. The only foolproof way to know how hot a chilli is, is to taste it. Nick a tiny bit off and eat it. Sometimes, large green chillies have almost no firepower in their flesh but loads in the seeds. Again, whether or not you use the seeds is up to you and how hot you want the dish to be. I like it to be fiery hot, rich and oily, and I then use small amounts of it to accompany milder dishes, like the pumpkin and spring cabbage dolma on page 124. To make this a more substantial dish, it will happily take some green vegetables on board – leeks, green beans, okra and spinach all work very well. Once, I made it into a kind of inverted pilaff by adding a few spoonfuls of cooked couscous at the end, not enough to change it to a grain dish but just enough to absorb any spare liquids.

FOR FOUR TO SIX:

- 200g chickpeas
- 1 onion, finely chopped
- 100mls olive oil
- 2–4 fresh chillies
- 2 tomatoes, deseeded
- 2 tsps cumin seeds
- 1 tsp salt
- 100mls tomato passata
- fresh coriander

SOAK THE CHICKPEAS OVERNIGHT and boil them until tender. This can take from one to three hours, depending on their age, but remember that chickpeas never get mushy-soft like lentils or other beans.

Start cooking the onion slowly in a couple of tablespoonfuls of the olive oil. Halve the chillies lengthways, then slice them into thin half-rounds. Chop the tomatoes into small dice, then add them to the pan with the chillies and the cumin seeds. Fry gently for a minute before adding the cooked chickpeas, the olive oil, salt and passata, and enough water to barely cover everything. Bring it to a boil, then cook at a lively simmer until the water is gone and the chickpeas have taken on a rich, oily sheen. Stir in lots of fresh coriander just before serving.

Sesame-fried cabbage

A great dish for propping up, physically and flavourwise, Asian flavoured pastries, fritters and the like. I like to use a lot of onion with the cabbage, sometimes close to equal quantities. One small cabbage will feed six people easily, in a supporting role to spring rolls or fritters. This one has to be for Patty Cremin, who was frying cabbage many years ago when it was neither fashionable nor profitable, though I never saw a bottle of sesame oil in her kitchen.

FOR FOUR:

- ½ small head savoy, spring or other cabbage
- 1 onion
- 2 tsps sesame seeds
- 1 tsp toasted sesame oil
- 1 tblspn soya sauce

CHOP THE CABBAGE into fairly thin strips, and the onion into thin quarter-rounds. Dry roast the seeds in a heavy pan, stirring occasionally, until very lightly browned. They will start to pop and fly out of the pan, which is why you can't really do them in the oven! I sometimes cook the cabbage in boiling water for a minute before frying it, especially hard, dry cabbages like savoy. Others, like spring greens, Chinese leaves and pak choy, are easy to fry from raw.

Heat some oil to a high temperature in a wok and cook the onion in it for a minute before adding the cabbage. Continue cooking and stirring for a few minutes, the time will depend on the cabbage you're using. An occasional splash of water will help to cook the cabbage, but be careful, too much will slow the cooking to something more like boiling than frying. Just as you judge the cabbage to be done – it should have softened but still be green – toss in a little soya sauce, then turn off the heat and stir in the sesame seeds and the sesame oil.

Fragrant basmati rice

A good-quality basmati rice has such an exquisite fragrance and flavour in its own right that you don't want to mess with it too much. This recipe, which we've always served with the tofu-cashew fritters on page 128, simply adds a few subtle flavours which go well with the coconut-stewed vegetables that also accompany the fritters.

FOR FOUR TO SIX:

- 400g basmati rice
- ½ tsp fennel seeds
- ½ tsp black mustard seeds
- ½ tsp yellow mustard seeds
- rind and juice of 1 lime
- ½ tsp salt
- 700mls boiling water

OVER A MEDIUM HEAT toss the rice and the seeds in a little oil for a few minutes, then add in the rest of the ingredients and stir until the water comes back to the boil – this will take only a few seconds. Cover and simmer on very low heat for 10 minutes. Leave undisturbed for a further two to five minutes, before uncovering and fluffing up the rice with a fork.

Lemon-buttered couscous

The classic way to cook couscous, by steaming it in muslin over the stew it will accompany, thus absorbing some of the stew's flavours, is very tricky for a restaurant to pull off, certainly for a restaurant not specializing in couscous – in the same way that pizza is very difficult to graft successfully on to a mixed-culture menu, and is done best by specialists. There is an excellent instruction on steaming couscous in a book called *A Mediterranean Harvest* by Paola Scaravelli and Jon Cohen which will either charm you or scare you off for life. Well, I admit I don't steam my couscous. Below is a description of what I do, taking 'lemon-buttered couscous' as a simple example. It is a very effective, and easy to control, way to prepare couscous – you get the flavours you want into it, some in the soaking, others at the end. If you want the couscous to have a specific or mixed vegetable flavour, use a stock for the soaking, or the reduced cooking water of a vegetable – fennel and asparagus work very well like that. One of my favourite things to add to couscous is the chermoula on page 35, which has such a complex taste that you simply use water to soak the grain and stir in the chermoula afterwards. The same would apply to, say, couscous with coriander-lime oil or with chilli-butter etc. Couscous, like pasta, loves both butter and olive oil, so the choice is up to you.

FOR FOUR TO SIX:

- 500g couscous
- rind and juice of 1 lemon
- a few strands of saffron
- 450mls hot water or light stock
- 50g butter
- salt
- pinch of cayenne pepper

PREPARE THE COUSCOUS 15 MINUTES before serving. In a large bowl, stir the lemon rind into the couscous, add the juice and the saffron to the hot water and stir this into the couscous. Some brands of couscous (it is a processed food, like pasta) seem to take more water, up to equal quantities (mls to grams), but be careful: you can't get the water back out if it's too much! Leave to soak for about 15 minutes, then fluff it up with a fork or your fingers. Chop the butter into small dice and stir it into the couscous with the seasoning. The couscous will still be warm, but if you want it hotter there are two things you can do. One is a brief steaming; the grains will be bigger now and shouldn't fall through a fine sieve. The other is a quick blast in a microwave. If the couscous is not to be stirred into a stew or roasted, as in the pilaff on page 117, it is very difficult to reheat any other way – you can't apply water to it unless you want porridge.

Felafel

Felafel, in its traditional guise, is a Middle-Eastern pitta bread sandwich filling. It seems to have crossed over into European cooking through vegetarian books and restaurants, where it has become as ubiquitous as melon on a hotel menu. This is one of those recipes that has evolved over the years and, yes I know, it's not the traditional way to make felafel. Think of it as a deep-fried chickpea fritter and a whole range of variations opens up. The basic recipe below will accommodate extra chilli, different spices or herbs, even some added nuts or finely chopped vegetables. Then the fritters formerly known as felafel can be served in all sorts of company. A few scattered on the plate with otherwise all-in-one dishes, like the root vegetable and couscous pilaff on page 117, gives the dish an extra focal point. They fit in very well in an Indian meal with a few subtle additions to the spices and they make a great snack food, dipped into a yoghurt or chilli sauce or their fellow-chickpeas-in-disguise, hummus.

FOR FOUR TO SIX:

- 250g chickpeas, soaked overnight
- 5 cloves garlic
- 1 tblspn cumin seeds, ground
- ½ tsp chopped chillies
- 250mls water
- 1 small onion, finely chopped or grated
- 250g gram flour
- 1 tsp salt
- juice of ½ lemon
- ½ tsp bread soda

COOK THE CHICKPEAS in plenty of boiling water until they are tender, allowing for the fact that chickpeas never cook to soft like other beans or lentils. Still, it can take from one to three hours to be satisfied that a chickpea has given up the ghost. Put the cooked chickpeas in a food processor with the garlic and spices, and blend them to a coarse powder, then add the water and blend again briefly to get a slightly coarse puree. Transfer this to a bowl and stir in the onion, gram flour, salt and lemon juice. You may need to sieve the gram flour – it always seems to be lumpy. Don't add the soda until just before you fry the felafel.

To cook the felafel, stir the soda into the batter, then drop teaspoonfuls of the batter into hot oil, carefully pushing it off with your finger or another spoon. If you have temperature control over your deep-frying oil, about 180°C/350°F is good. The felafel will puff up in the cooking and you may need to turn them once. Cooked ones will keep warm in a low oven while you cook more.

Green pepper-coriander salsa

We use this for the carrot, almond and feta terrine on page 74. Because the vegetables are left raw, rather than the method used in the fennel-chilli salsa, I chop them much smaller, using a food processor to get what could be called finely chopped or a coarse puree texture.

FOR FOUR TO SIX:

- 2 green peppers
- 1 red onion
- 2 cloves of garlic
- juice of ½ lime
- salt
- pinch of cayenne pepper
- fresh coriander, chopped
- 2 tomatoes, deseeded
- 3–4 tablspns olive oil

COARSELY CHOP THE PEPPERS, onion and garlic, put them in a food processor and reduce them to a coarse puree. Transfer this to a bowl and stir in the lime juice, seasoning, some chopped fresh coriander and the tomatoes, finely diced. Finally, stir in enough olive oil to make the salsa slightly wet.

Fennel-chilli salsa

These two go together really well, even for people who claim to dislike fennel. I think it's that sweetness/chilli-heat combination again, one of my favourite food tastes at the moment. The brief cooking time given below is one of the few strict times I use. You're not really trying to cook anything, it's just to take the sharp rawness off the onion, garlic, chilli and fennel while leaving them crunchy. We use this for the corn pancakes on page 72, but like most salsas it is as adaptable as you want it to be. It keeps well for a few days, but the flavours do blur into a single taste, rather than the vibrant, contrasting flavours of their first day together.

FOR FOUR TO SIX:

- 1 medium fennel bulb
- 1 small red onion
- 2 tomatoes, deseeded
- 2 cloves of garlic
- 1 or 2 fresh chillies
- 3–4 tblspns olive oil
- 1 tsp balsamic vinegar
- salt
- some chopped fresh parsley and fennel

THE QUANTITIES OF FENNEL, red onion and tomato should be roughly similar when prepared – do the fennel first and match the others to that. Coarse outer leaves of fennel may have to be discarded, though the inner core is often edible, especially when chopped very finely and stewed. Dice the fennel, red onion and garlic. Deseed the chillies and slice them thinly – how many you use depends on their heat and your own taste. Pour in about three tablespoons of olive oil, over a moderate heat, cook the fennel, onion, garlic and chillies for two minutes, then remove this immediately to a bowl. Add the rest of the ingredients, using enough olive oil to give a slightly wet consistency. Allow to cool to room temperature before serving.

Avocado salsa

- 2 tomatoes, deseeded
- 1 red onion
- 2 cloves of garlic
- 1 fresh chilli, deseeded
- pinch of salt
- juice of one lime
- fresh coriander
- 3–4 tblspns olive oil
- 1 avocado

CHOP THE TOMATOES into small dice. Finely chop the onion, garlic and chilli and combine all the ingredients except the avocado in a bowl. A short time before serving, chop all the avocado flesh into dice similar to the tomato, and stir into the salsa.

Harissa-sweet pepper oil

This oil-as-sauce was first put together for the root vegetable and couscous pilaff on page 117. The pilaff is flavoured with the complex but low-key tastes of our chermoula so we came up with this oil to add a dramatic element to the mix. It's a combination I love: sweet, rich and very hot. It's hard to say how many this recipe serves, but it makes 600mls. Depending on the chilli-heat level and your fondness for it, this could feed eight to fifteen people. I like it to be very hot in which case a little gives a big hit, but if you make it a bit milder it's a pleasure to mop up loads of it. Up to you. The finished oil will keep very well for up to a week in a fridge.

- 2 red peppers, roasted and peeled
- 250mls olive oil
- 150mls water
- 5 tsps harissa paste

COARSELY CHOP THE PEPPERS and put them in a pan with the olive oil, water and harissa. Bring to the boil and keep at a rolling boil for two minutes. Leave to cool for a few minutes only, then blend it using a hand blender or food processor – the hand blender works better. Most times you will get an emulsion that will last for ever, but occasionally the components gradually become separate again – don't worry, just give it a quick blend or whisk before serving. Leave the oil to cool before serving, though it tastes fine warm too.

Pineapple chutney

We use this mildly spiced sweet chutney with the tofu-cashew fritters on page 128. This recipe makes about 500mls, enough for eight to ten generous portions, but it's as easy to make double the quantity if you've got the pineapple.

- 1 onion
- 500g pineapple, fresh or tinned
- 150mls pineapple juice
- ¼ tsp salt
- 1 tsp ground cumin
- 1 tsp ground coriander
- 4 cloves ground
- ½ tsp cinnamon
- ½ tsp cayenne pepper
- ½ tsp nutmeg
- ½ tsp ground ginger
- 2 dstspns demerara sugar
- juice and rind of ½ lemon

FINELY CHOP THE ONION and the pineapple, either diligently by hand or carefully with the pulse function of a food processor. Put them in a heavy pan with the other ingredients and simmer, covered, over a low heat for 30 minutes, stirring occasionally. If it then seems too wet, turn up the heat and cook it, uncovered, at a brisk boil for a few minutes more. Leave the chutney to cool completely before using. Stored in an airtight container in a fridge, it will keep for up to ten days.

Chermoula

Since I first discovered and adapted a recipe for this complex seasoning, I have come across dozens more wildly different versions. So, though I still like this recipe, it is obviously flexible and open to personal interpretation. I think of the three herbs, the cumin and the paprika as the core of the flavour, though I suspect you could get a good result with just one of the herbs too. Chermoula combines brilliantly with grains, especially couscous. A well-balanced chermoula seems to become one flavour, though not one that people can recognise; this can be used as the dominant taste of a couscous dish or in small amounts to act as the base for other spices. A couscous pilaff might start with a light coating of chermoula on the grains, then have whole toasted cumin or coriander seeds, fresh coriander and even fresh chillies added to the mix. These up-front, heady flavours shine out while the chermoula holds the basic tone of the dish. As a guide, one or two dessertspoons per person will liven up any couscous or rice dish.

- 1 tsp cumin seeds
- 1 tsp fennel seeds
- 50g coriander
- 100g parsley
- 30g mint
- 3 cloves garlic
- 3 tsps paprika
- ¼ tsp cayenne pepper
- ½ tsp salt
- rind of ½ lemon, grated
- rind of ½ orange, grated
- 300mls olive oil

PUT THE CUMIN and fennel seeds in a heavy frying pan over a low heat for a few minutes until lightly toasted, then grind them in an electric grinder or a mortar and pestle. Put the herbs and garlic in a food processor and chop them finely, then add the rest of the ingredients and blend them briefly to a thickish pesto-like consistency.

Black olive tapenade

It might sound rudely obvious, but your tapenade will taste of the olives it is made from. Therefore, one made from tasteless supermarket stoned olives and cheap oil will be, well, tasteless. If you can't find a source of well-flavoured stoned olives, do it yourself. It can be fun. Put the olives on a chopping board, lay the flat of a large knife blade or a smaller board or suchlike on top, then pound this a few times with your fist. The stones should now pop out easily. We use tapenade mostly in its original thick form, spread on sandwich bread or between grilled crusty bread and goats' cheese as a snack. It has also been occasionally thinned with olive oil for a dressing, as on page 45 and as a sauce for polenta.

- 3 cloves garlic
- 250g stoned black olives
- 2 tsps capers
- 25g sundried tomatoes, chopped
- pinch of cayenne pepper
- 150mls olive oil

PUT EVERYTHING EXCEPT the oil in a food processor and blend to a coarse puree, then add the oil and blend again briefly. Store the tapenade in an airtight container with a thin layer of olive oil above the puree, preferably in the fridge, and it will keep for weeks.

Pesto

Basil pesto is a classic sauce, a balanced union of perfectly harmonious ingredients. The recipe here is, I think, a fairly standard one; it certainly makes a delicious and endlessly useful sauce for pasta, risotto, omelettes, fritters, roasted vegetables, grilled cheeses, in or over sandwiches and so on. There are those who would say that basil pesto is the pesto and that's that, no messing will be tolerated. I would very nearly be with them, except that I am guilty of a little messing myself. The other pesto recipes here have served me well and I give them with confidence. Herb pesto keeps well for up to a week, maybe a little longer, but the flavours become a little flabby and dulled, whereas freshly made pesto is vibrant. It is a good way to preserve fresh herb flavours if your access to herbs is only sporadic.

Basil pesto

- 100g basil
- 50g pinenuts, lightly toasted
- 2 cloves of garlic
- salt and pepper
- 200–250mls olive oil
- 40g parmesan, grated

PUT EVERYTHING EXCEPT THE OIL and cheese in a food processor and blend to a coarse puree. Add half the oil and the parmesan and blend again for a few seconds. Transfer the pesto to a jug or bowl and stir in the rest of the oil, or as much of it as you think the pesto needs. Different dishes need their accompanying pesto at different consistencies, so I think it is best to store the pesto thick and dilute it with olive oil when and as you wish. Keep a thin film of olive oil on top of the stored pesto, to help preserve the colour.

For basil pesto dressing, simply take a few spoons of the pesto, dilute it to a pouring consistency with olive oil, then add some lemon juice to taste.

Rocket pesto

An identical recipe to the basil classic, this has the peppery flavour of rocket which is just as happy in the company of pinenuts, garlic, olive oil and parmesan as basil is, and can be used in the same way.

- 100g rocket
- 50g pinenuts, lightly toasted
- 2 cloves of garlic
- salt and pepper
- 200–250mls olive oil
- 40g parmesan, grated

PUT EVERYTHING EXCEPT THE OIL and cheese in a food processor and blend to a coarse puree. Add half the oil and the parmesan and blend again for a few seconds. Transfer the pesto to a jug or bowl and stir in the rest of the oil, or as much of it as you think the pesto needs. As with other pesto, store it thick and dilute with olive oil when needed. Store with a thin film of olive oil on top.

Coriander-chilli pesto

Based on the basil recipe, but with a very different character, this was made initially for the pumpkin, almond and spring cabbage dolma on page 124, and is best with Middle-Eastern or North African-style dishes.

- 100g coriander
- 40g ground almonds
- 2 cloves of garlic
- 1 fresh green chilli or 2 small dried chillies
- ¼ salt
- 200–250mls olive oil

PUT EVERYTHING except the oil and in a food processor and blend to a coarse puree. Add half the oil and blend again, briefly. Transfer the pesto to a jug or bowl and stir in the rest of the oil, or as much of it as you think the pesto needs. The same instructions on storing and use apply here as for the other pesto recipes.

Sundried tomato pesto

This is hardly a pesto at all, if you think of a pesto as having cheese, nuts and herbs as the main ingredients. But it does have olive oil as the liquid component and it is used like a pesto - as a sauce, a dressing on pasta, a spread on bread and crostini etc. This basic recipe will easily take on board other flavours: herbs, chillies, the classic pesto tastes of pinenuts and parmesan. One of my favourite uses for this is as stored sunshine in a sauce for winter foods, like the spinach, leek and stilton tart on page 111.

- 80g sundried tomatoes
- 2 cloves garlic
- large pinch of cayenne pepper
- ¼ tsp salt
- juice of ½ lemon
- 200–250mls olive oil

SOAK THE TOMATOES in just enough hot water to cover them for 20 minutes, then drain off the liquid. If you foresee yourself making any soups, sauces, stews or the like in the immediate future that would benefit from some sweetish tomato water, save the liquid, otherwise pour it away. Put all the ingredients in a food processor and blend to a coarse puree. Pour in the olive oil and blend briefly. As with the tapenade, store the pesto as a thick puree, with a thin layer of olive oil on top, leaving you the option of diluting it to suit its many uses.

Basil oil, rosemary-chilli oil and coriander-lime oil

There is an increasing variety of flavoured and infused oils for sale in supermarkets and food shops. The worst are thin and insipid, too delicate and use poor oil to start with. The best, or the ones I like most, are made from good olive oil, the rich flavour of which is enhanced by the intense, aromatic herbs and/or spices added. There is something very exotic about these bottled miracles of flavour; an impression of alchemy, something that could only be conjured in the room behind the shop of some old Tuscan oil merchant. This may well be the case for all I know, since I've rarely been happy with my occasional attempts at infusion. However, at Café Paradiso there are always at hand at least two of our own flavoured oils and two or three others – if you count toasted sesame, which I would never be without, and other nut oils (less essential but nice to know they are there). At the moment there are, let's see, ten different oils in the kitchen. Spoiled, aren't we? I'll tell you how we 'make' three of these and some things we use them for, though whether these instructions could be called recipes is doubtful.

Basil oil

This is a staple at Café Paradiso, always to hand to add richness and flavour. For pasta it is a sauce in itself; for puy lentils, broad beans with roasted garlic, new potatoes, sprouting broccoli or anything simply cooked, basil oil can be added towards the end of cooking or tossed with the vegetables afterwards. The oil is used from the start in stewing peppers for peperonata, and for wilting various greens. It goes into salad dressings, mayonnaise and aioli, is drizzled over risotto and egg dishes. A bowl of it at room temperature is perfect for dunking fresh bread into. This is not a long-life infused oil; it is a fresh product with a shelf life of a couple of weeks, mainly because of how we make it, leaving all the basil bits in. We make batches every few days, so I see no point in throwing the basil out. If you want to go for a longer shelf life you could, after a few days, strain the basil off through a fine sieve or muslin.

- 500mls olive oil
- 1 handful basil leaves and stalk

DISCARD ANY VERY COARSE or poor quality stalk, then put the rest in a food processor and chop it finely, but only for a short time as too much will pulverise and blacken the basil, especially if the blades aren't as sharp as they once were. Now pour in the olive oil and blend briefly. The result should be simply an olive oil flecked with tiny bits of bright green basil. Store the oil in a lidded jar or bottle, not necessarily in the fridge, though this will add a few days to its life.

Rosemary-chilli oil

We make this in a way much closer to 'proper' infusion. Rinse and dry a few sprigs of fresh rosemary and a few whole dried chillies – those large, red, mildish ones are good for this but if you want more heat use the tiny Thai 'bird's eye' or even a 'habanero' if you can find one. Put them into a litre of good olive oil put the lid on and leave it for a couple of days. The flavours will get stronger for a few days, then level off. The oil will hold the flavour for ages, you can even top it up as the level goes down, but after a couple of weeks there will be nothing more to take from the rosemary and chillies, so take them out. This method also works very well with sprigs of thyme.

This is a much less multi-purpose oil than the basil, because of the two very individual and dominating flavours in it. They get on beautifully together and with olive oil, but after that you need to be careful where you let them go. It is excellent as a bread dip or a pasta sauce for tomatoes, aubergines, kale, onions (not necessarily all together), and brilliant with goats' cheese or eggs. There is a recipe on page 40 (below) for a roasted garlic-rosemary aioli which is, for the ones who love those flavours, the most heavenly dip for dunking into with whatever is to hand - raw vegetables, fried fritters, bread, cold potatoes late at night ...

Coriander-lime oil

This one we concocted for a specific dish, the coconut-cumin pancakes on page 109. It's made in the same way as the basil oil and the same storage instructions apply. Take a half litre of olive oil, blend it with a handful of washed coriander and the grated rind of one lime. The combination of coriander and lime give a light, heady and fresh sheen to a dish with lots of intense, long-cooked flavours and dense starchy foods.

Aioli from herb oils

Aioli, in French, or alioli in Spanish, is a garlic sauce, emulsion or mayonnaise made with olive oil. That's all. While a strong olive oil can be too much, even nasty, in a mayonnaise for dressing salads, it is brilliant with garlic as a dip. The traditional sauces use raw garlic, but as I get older I seem to not want to smell like that too often any more, especially as it is also the smell of my work coming from my every pore at the end of the day. That said, I've become addicted to roasted garlic. This recipe can be made with any olive oil but I love these flavours together: rosemary, chilli, roasted garlic, fruity olive oil. Crying out for a potato, they are. Oh, I must point out that using a whole egg to make mayonnaise only works with a food processor. If you prefer to use the traditional method, use only the egg yolk.

- 6–8 cloves garlic
- a little olive oil
- 1 egg
- 250mls rosemary-chilli oil
- salt and pepper
- a little lemon juice if you like

SNIP THE ROOT END OFF each of the garlic cloves but leave the skins on. Toss the cloves in olive oil and roast them in the oven at about 320–350°F (Gas Mark 3–4) until they are soft. The garlic flesh will squeeze out easily at the snipped end. Put the garlic in a food processor with the egg and blend them for a minute. Then, still blending, slowly pour in the rosemary oil, which should emulsify with the egg to give you a thick mayonnaise. Season it and add a little lemon juice if you feel the need. If the result is too thin, simply add more oil until you get what you want. If, by any chance, the thing doesn't emulsify at all and you have a separated mess, put the mess in a jug, clean the machine thoroughly, beat another egg in it for a minute and use the mess as an oil, pouring it in slowly and steadily until, this time, you get what you want.

Polenta

The colour alone, lightly scorched corn-yellow, is a good reason to put a wedge of grilled polenta on a plate. Add to that the sunshine of roasted peppers or the vivid greens of wilted chard, sprouting broccoli or fresh rocket and you can hardly go wrong. At Paradiso we always make 'set' polenta for grilling or frying, but if you want to serve the polenta fresh and 'wet' add extra water at the start and cook for the same length of time. Remember that it is only porridge made from maize and takes a lot of seasoning and added flavours to make it interesting. I generally use a simple polenta as a foil for dishes rich in olive oil, dairy produce or spices. The recipe below is for the polenta most often made at Paradiso and is only lightly seasoned with chilli and oregano, to be served as a starter or with the likes of the aubergine gamelastra on page 133. This quantity will fill a standard Swiss-roll tray to a thickness of about 15mm, which would feed eight to twelve people. It is a simple matter to make the polenta thicker or thinner as you fancy, or to make less by using a smaller container; indeed it doesn't need a container and could simply be spread on a chopping board or worktop. The corn I use is sold as 'coarse maize' and the times and water quantities below work for this. If you use a product called 'polenta' or 'instant polenta' just follow the instructions on the pack. They are all essentially the same thing – corn or maize.

- 1.2 litres water or stock
- 300g coarse maize
- 1 tsp salt
- ¼ tsp chopped dried chillies
- 1 tsp dried oregano

BRING THE STOCK TO THE BOIL in a large pot. Sift the other ingredients together, then quickly whisk them into the boiling liquid. As soon as it comes back to the boil, turn down the heat and swap the whisk for a wooden spoon. Polenta, like porridge can splatter volcanically at this stage, so be careful. Simmer the polenta for about 12 minutes, stirring often. It will become thick and gloopy quickly making it difficult to decide when it is cooked; generally I simply give it the allotted time and then take it off the heat. Line a Swiss-roll tray with baking parchment, or lightly oil the tray, and quickly spread the polenta into it. Use a dampened pallet knife, rolling pin or the palm of your hand to give it a smooth finish. Alternatively, simply spread it on a worktop or chopping board and level it as best you can. Leave the polenta to cool and set for half an hour or so, then turn it out and slice it into the shapes you want to use. The recipe on page 45 is a basic model for a simple starter of grilled polenta.

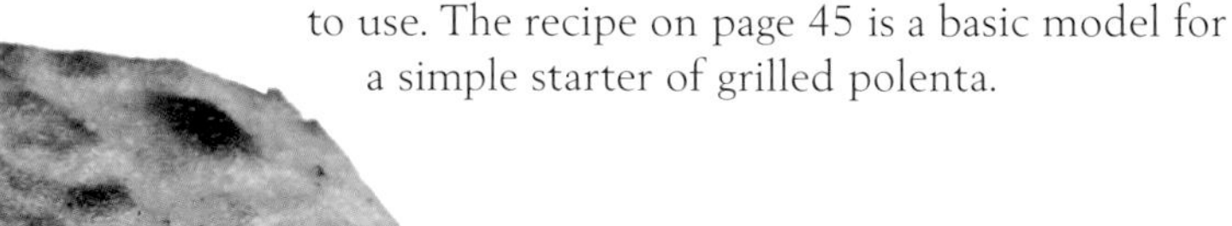

Starters

Grilled polenta ¶ Bridget's salad ¶ Salad Tobias ¶ Summer vegetables with mixed leaves ¶ Rocket and flat-leaf parsley salad ¶ Broad bean, spinach and beetroot salad ¶ Thai cucumber and green bean salad ¶ Watercress, new potato and avocado salad ¶ Tomato salad ¶ Tempura ¶ Roasted tomato soup ¶ Chilled beetroot soup ¶ Celeriac, potato and hazelnut soup ¶ Purple sprouting broccoli with new potatoes ¶ Deep-fried courgette flower parcels of sheep's cheese and pinenuts ¶ Roasted pepper, olive and brie tartlets ¶ Beetroot mousse ¶ Pan-fried parmesan-stuffed artichoke fritters ¶ Oyster mushroom and smoked Gubeen ravioli ¶ Braised spinach parcels of feta, green pepper and caramelized onion ¶ Aubergine sticky rice rolls ¶ Corn pancakes of roasted pepper, red onion and goats' cheese ¶ Carrot, almond and feta terrine ¶ Peperonata with olive-grilled ciabatta ¶ Asparagus and Gabriel cheese gratin ¶ Three wontons in a ginger broth ¶ Leek and pinenut timbale ¶ Deep-fried salsify and celeriac fritters ¶ Oyster mushrooms ¶ Gingered sweet potato spring roll ¶

Grilled polenta

with olive tapenade, parmesan and rocket

This is the simplest version of this dish. Other variations I use a lot include replacing the raw rocket with wilted chard or black kale, lightly cooked asparagus or purple sprouting broccoli. Basil or rocket pesto can also be used instead of the tapenade.

FOR FOUR:

- ½ batch of polenta recipe on page 41
- 2 tblspns tapenade (see page 35)
- 2 tblspns olive oil
- 200g rocket
- 1 piece parmesan, about 60g

CUT THE COOLED POLENTA INTO EIGHT TRIANGULAR WEDGES, brush these on both sides with olive oil and cook under a hot grill, or on a griddle pan, until they become crisp on the outside and start to brown. Turn the wedges once to cook both sides evenly.

Dilute the tapenade with the olive oil. Put a couple of polenta wedges on each of four plates and pour the tapenade around them. Top with a generous handful of rocket and use a potato peeler to shave the parmesan over everything.

Bridget's salad

- organic salad leaves
- fresh herbs
- olive oil
- balsamic vinegar
- black pepper

Bridget goes through a small allotment's worth of salad leaves every day – with meals, before meals, instead of meals, crammed into bread rolls at the beach ... This is the mother of all salads; it's on every restaurant menu and in every home, in some shape or form. So often it is the best and most appropriate start to a meal, especially when there's a lot of rich food on the way; and its preparation, I think, is the essence of good food. There are no impressive techniques to hide behind, no artful presentation. A generous helping of quality ingredients is the only way to please. The Bridget method involves roughly tearing up whatever leaves are available; the more the merrier (up to a point) but even one good fresh organic lettuce is fine, using the basic, blander varieties as the bulk and stronger leaves, like rocket, sorrel, mizuna, cresses and the like, left whole and used more sparingly. The same goes for herbs – only parsley and, to a lesser extent, basil can be flung in by the handful. While Bridget will occasionally go to the trouble of making a dressing, usually it's a case of pouring on some fine olive oil, a good splash of balsamic vinegar and a hefty grinding of pepper. Always prepare a generous amount of leaves, but only dress as much as you think will be eaten immediately – it's only a few seconds' work to dress another batch.

Salad Tobias

This salad has been around, in one form or another, since Café Paradiso opened. It is essentially a basic green salad with interesting bits added to make a more substantial starter or light lunch. It got its name from Toby the olive man, because at first all of the ingredients except the lettuce came from his stall in Cork's English Market. This is the current version but other former stars include roasted peppers, potatoes, green beans, parmesan or sheep's cheese shavings and, of course, olives. We make the mayonnaise quite thick and intense, and dilute it as required - a thick dressing will weigh down a salad. (The original thick version makes a lovely dip for warm asparagus.) For the fresh herbs use parsley, basil and thyme as a base, and one or two of oregano, dill, marjoram, fennel, chervil or chives.

FOR FOUR:

- 2 cloves of garlic
- fresh herbs
- 1 egg
- 1 tsp Dijon mustard
- 300mls sunflower oil
- 2 tblspns white wine vinegar
- salt and pepper
- hot water
- a handful of croutons
- salad leaves, 2–4 types, equivalent to 2 small lettuce heads
- 8 artichoke hearts
- 4 tsps of capers
- 8 dried or semi-dried tomatoes

COARSELY CHOP THE GARLIC AND HERBS, then put them in a food processor to finely chop them. Add the egg and mustard and leave the processor running for a minute or two. While it is running, start to slowly pour in the sunflower oil and keep pouring until you have a thick emulsion. Add most of the vinegar and some seasoning, blend briefly, then taste the mayonnaise. You may need to add more seasoning or vinegar. This quantity will be too much for your Tobias salad, and it will be too thick. To dilute the mayonnaise for this salad, whisk in some hot water – it doesn't take much to change the thick emulsion to a pouring consistency. The rest will keep for up to a week in the fridge.

To make the croutons, cut some day-old bread into small dice, toss these in olive oil in an oven tray and bake at a moderate temperature for about ten minutes, until nicely toasted and crisp.

Toss the leaves in enough mayonnaise to coat them and divide between four plates. Quarter or halve the artichokes and scatter them on top of the greens with the capers, tomatoes and croutons. Drizzle a little more mayonnaise over the salad, aiming for the unadorned vegetables.

Summer vegetables with mixed leaves,

pesto dressing and Knockalara sheep's cheese

Now and then, when the organic vegetables are coming in vividly fresh and young, we put a selection of them on as a starter, to give them a chance to show themselves off at their finest. Rather than a jumbled salad, which this potentially is, I like to present the different vegetables in separate piles to give them room to shine. This is really a grower's dish, and the most important thing for the cook to do in such fine company is to have respect, pay attention to the qualities of each vegetable and then decide how best to prepare each one. The combination below is on the menu this week as I write in early summer and includes one grilled vegetable, one boiled, two barely shown the water, and some raw leaves and garlic flowers. I include slices of Knockalara sheep's cheese from Cappoquin in Co. Waterford because its fresh, mildly tangy flavour is redolent of early summer in the same way as the vegetables are. But you don't need a cheese, and a lot of other vegetables would love the chance to shine: roasted young beetroot and fennel bulbs, new potatoes, fresh young cauliflower, beans and peas of all kinds, fresh sweetcorn and plum tomatoes. The only requirement is that they are in peak condition. The asparagus used here would be delicious grilled or roasted, and the artichoke would be fine just boiled and tossed in oil; I don't really like more than one grilled flavour on the plate, it can detract from that hardly touched effect you want the vegetables to have.

FOR FOUR:

- 4 artichokes
- juice of ½ lemon
- 8–12 asparagus spears
- 8–12 baby carrots
- 20–30 sugar snaps
- 2 tblspns basil pesto (see page 37)
- 2–3 tblspns olive oil
- salad leaves, equal to 1 small lettuce head
- balsamic vinegar
- 120g Knockalara sheep's cheese, thickly sliced
- small bunch of wild garlic, leaves and flowers

TRIM ALL LEAVES FROM THE ARTICHOKES and remove the hairy choke – rub lemon juice all over the revealed artichoke bottom as you work, to prevent discolouring. Boil the artichoke bottoms in water to which more lemon juice has been added for 10–20 minutes until they are just done – test with a knife. Sometime within half an hour or so before serving, brush the artichokes with olive oil and place under a hot grill or in a hot fan oven, until lightly browned. They're best eaten at something between warm and room temperature.

Snap the coarse ends off the asparagus, then drop the spears into boiling water until they are just tender. Rinse briefly in cold water to stop the cooking without actually making the asparagus cold. Both the baby carrots and sugar snaps are edible raw, so how much you cook them is up to you. I would give the carrots a minute at most in boiling water, and either leave the sugar snaps raw or drop them in boiling water for as long as it takes to do a slow pirouette. To make a dressing from the basil pesto, simply dilute with olive oil, then add lemon juice to taste.

Place a small pile of salad leaves – use only two or three types at most – in the centre of each of four plates, dressed in a little olive oil and balsamic vinegar, maybe, then arrange little piles of the various vegetables and cheese around. Scatter some garlic flowers and chopped leaves over the plate and pour a thin stream of the dressing over the cheese and vegetables.

Rocket and flat-leaf parsley salad

with currants, parmesan, a balsamic dressing and tomato crostini

Rocket defies fashion like nothing else that has been subjected to such overuse, misuse, abuse and downright misspelling. It's been picked from the wild and cultivated for aeons by people who eat for pleasure and, like all the most interesting vegetables, can vary widely in flavour depending on its age and place of birth. Young, early-spring rocket, or tunnel-grown, is delicate, pale and subtle; later on, when the leaves are bigger, darker and tougher, it can be peppery, pungent and bitter. Some people have an ideal rocket and while I tend towards the more mature and robust, I love to follow its changes and make adjustments to how I treat it. This recipe needs a strong-flavoured rocket to cope with the various sweet, sharp and peppery flavours. It is an evolved salad, taking one element from a dinner I had at Chez Panisse in San Francisco, a couple from home and one from an otherwise awful meal in Dublin, which I can't bring myself to credit. The parmesan mixed into the salad lifts it to a higher level, because if there's one thing rocket loves, young or old, it's fresh parmesan. The essence of this salad, the one we eat at home, is rocket, parmesan, olive oil and balsamic vinegar, eaten using fingers as cutlery, of course.

FOR FOUR:

- 1 tblspn currants
- 200g rocket
- 100g flat-leaf parsley
- 1 small red onion
- 20g parmesan, finely grated
- black pepper
- 80mls olive oil
- 2 tblspns balsamic vinegar
- 2 cloves of garlic
- 20g parmesan, whole, for shaving
- 4 slices of day-old bread, preferably focaccia
- 2 tblspns tomato pesto (see page 38)

SOAK THE CURRANTS IN HOT WATER – just enough to cover them – for 20 minutes, then drain off the water. Pick through the rocket and parsley to sort out any unworthy leaves and tough stalks. Leave the rocket leaves whole and tear the parsley stalks into manageable pieces, about the size of the rocket leaves. Slice the red onion very thinly in half-rounds, and gently mix it into the rocket with the currants, the grated parmesan and some coarsely ground black pepper.

To make the dressing, put the oil and vinegar in a jar, crush the garlic and add it in. Put a lid on the jar and shake it briskly for a few seconds. Use a whisk and jug if you prefer, but not an electric blender as the result will be too thick to do anything but sit on top of the salad. Toss the salad in the dressing, distribute it on to four plates and scatter a few shavings of parmesan over each one.

To make the crostini, first take any crust off the bread. The slices need to be about 10mm thick. Brush the slices generously on both sides with olive oil and put them in a moderate oven for about ten minutes. You may need to turn them once, though a fan oven will cook both sides evenly. The crostini are done, or at least done to my liking, when the slices are crisp on all sides while retaining some softness in the middle. They will keep for a few days in this condition in an airtight container.

To finish the crostini, spread a thin layer of tomato pesto on each slice and pop them back in the oven or under a grill just to warm them through. Cut the slices into small triangles, or any shape you want, and tuck a few crostini into each salad or put them on the table separately.

Broad bean, spinach and beetroot salad

with Ardsallagh goats' cheese and a tapenade dressing

I hope you can deal with the shock if I tell you that most of the stuff sold as salad spinach in this country isn't true spinach at all. It is a cruder, hardier, perpetual variety that is plentiful, easy to grow and excellent for cooking. Salad spinach should be soft, delicate and meltingly buttery in the mouth. This is a late spring salad that teams the spinach with young broad beans, fresh beetroot and a mild fresh goats' cheese from East Cork. If you replace this with another cheese, the character should be mildly goaty, soft, with a subtle fresh tang. Mind you, I've also used a hard, sharp, mature sheep's cheese to good effect here. Early season broad beans are small, cute and edible almost raw, but they gradually become fatter, thick skinned and floury as the season wears on. I love them that way too and would never bother peeling them, though it doesn't help to pass the mature off as young. When buying or picking broad beans, remember that you'll be lucky to get a third of the total weight; so here you'll need about 500g of bean pods. Frozen broad beans are often excellent, always small and cute and don't lose any weight!

FOR FOUR:

- 4 medium-sized beetroots
- 150g broad beans
- 400g baby spinach leaves
- 4 tblspns olive oil
- juice of ½ lemon
- 2 tblspns tapenade (see page 35)
- 2 spring onions, chopped
- 100g Ardsallagh goats' cheese, or similar

BOIL THE BEETROOT IN PLENTY OF WATER until just cooked. This should take about half an hour, but can take much longer if the roots are old and stubborn. Under cold water, rub the outer skin off with your fingers; if it doesn't slip away easily, curse a little and take a knife to them. While the beetroot is cooking, prepare the other vegetables. Cook the beans in boiling water until tender (about eight minutes), but remember that frequent testing is the only way to know if they are cooked to your satisfaction. Carefully wash and dry the spinach leaves remembering that they bruise easily. Make a dressing by simply whisking the olive oil and lemon juice into the tapenade.

Slice each of the beetroots into four or six wedges, toss these in enough olive oil to coat them and roast them in a hot oven, turning them once or twice. While the roots are cooling a little, toss the spinach, broad beans and spring onions in enough dressing to coat them, then share these out among four plates and arrange the still-warm beetroot on the plates too. Break the cheese into a rough crumble of large and small pieces and scatter it generously and randomly over the salad. Drizzle some more dressing over the top.

Thai cucumber and green bean salad

with a roasted peanut-citrus dressing and crisped rice vermicelli

This salad, based on a recipe in an American book by Jacki Passmore, was a revelation to me. I was curious about it because it uses no oil, lots of sugar and yet promises palate-stimulating excitement. So we knocked up a variation of it, picked at it, and were quite taken aback by the way all these mouth-tingling flavours came together in such a perfect balance. It is probably the most refreshing starter we've ever featured, and certainly gets the hunger juices flowing, which is a cook's dream. Its appearance and ingredients do look a bit ordinary, like something from a supermarket deli, and it could easily taste that way too if you skip a few details. Make the dressing first, and prepare the vegetables shortly before you need them, but dress the salad only when it is about to be served. The fresh herbs are essential and in large quantities too – I don't really know how much a bunch of coriander weighs, just be generous. The crisped vermicelli are an added texture and can be left out without spoiling the effect of the salad.

FOR FOUR:

- corn or peanut oil
- 1 small handful of rice vermicelli
- 2 cucumbers
- 200g green beans
- 1 red pepper (optional – for colour only)
- 20g roasted unsalted peanuts
- ½–1 small head of Chinese leaves or crisp lettuce
- 1 large handful of fresh coriander, about 30g
- 1 small handful of fresh basil, about 15g

FOR THE DRESSING:

- 1 tblspn roasted unsalted peanuts
- 1 large mild red chilli, deseeded
- 100mls lime or lemon juice
- 2 dstspns light palm or soft brown sugar
- 1 clove of garlic, crushed

TO MAKE THE DRESSING, finely chop the peanuts by hand or food processor, but not a grinder – which will give you powder in seconds – and slice the chilli very finely. Then whisk these with the juice, sugar and garlic. You can do this with a hand whisk or, again, with a few short pulses of the food processor.

Heat about a 5cm depth of corn or peanut oil in a small saucepan until it is quite hot. Drop in the vermicelli, which will immediately begin to sizzle, brown and swell. This can be alarming for people not accustomed to drama in their kitchen. You may need to turn the vermicelli, so stand over the pan and remove the noodles as soon as they are lightly browned, which will only take a minute or so. Drain the noodles on paper and set them aside. This can be done any time on the day you want to use them, and they will even keep for a couple of days in an airtight container.

Peel the cucumbers, scoop out and discard the seeds, and slice them into thinnish pieces about 4cm long. Drop the green beans into boiling water for one or two minutes, depending on their age and thickness. Cool them immediately in cold water. Slice the red pepper into strips about half the thickness of the cucumber pieces. Coarsely chop or halve the peanuts, finely shred the Chinese leaves or lettuce and mix all the ingredients together. As a guide, the lettuce or leaves should be only half the volume of the other vegetables together. Pour the dressing over the vegetables and toss them briefly before piling the salad on to four plates. Sprinkle a little vermicelli over each portion.

Watercress, new potato and avocado salad

with a Spanish paprika and yoghurt dressing

We have an occasional supply of organic watercress from a pond on Hollyhill Farm in West Cork. When we get a consistent and abundant supply for a few weeks, I tend to experiment a little with it, but nothing works as well for me as a generous helping as a salad first course for dinner. Potatoes and watercress just love each other but the day we created this salad, the two things I was excited about were the watercress and a tin of Spanish paprika. (Well, what gets you excited?) The other ingredients practically volunteered themselves to make a salad combination of obvious but perfect partners. I consider the yoghurt to be acid enough for the dressing, but if you want more bite in it a little lemon juice would be fine.

FOR FOUR:

- 1 clove of garlic, crushed
- 100mls olive oil
- 100mls yoghurt
- 2 tsps paprika
- hot water
- salt and pepper to taste
- 400g new potatoes
- 300g watercress
- 1 bunch of spring onions
- 2 avocados

TO MAKE THE DRESSING, put the garlic in a jug with the olive oil, yoghurt and paprika. Whisk these together to get a fairly thick emulsion, either with a hand whisk or electric blender, then dilute this to the consistency of pouring cream by whisking in a little hot water. Season with salt and pepper.

Boil the potatoes until just cooked and cool them a little under cold water. Halve them if they are very small, or slice bigger ones fairly thickly. (Slicing the potatoes before cooking them works just as well and is also a little quicker.) Prepare the watercress by washing and drying it carefully, then pick through it to discard any dodgy leaves or woody stalk, bearing in mind that most of the stalk is edible. Tear the watercress into fairly big pieces – these will maintain a structure on the plate, where small pieces would fall flat and limp. Chop the spring onions, and toss them with the potatoes and watercress. Add some dressing and gently toss the salad to lightly coat the vegetables, then put a mound of salad on each of four plates. Cut the avocados in half and remove the stones, then scoop out the flesh in one piece with a spoon. Quickly, slice the halves into thickish pieces, then tuck these into the salads. Drizzle a little more dressing over any parts of the salads that look a little bare or neglected.

Tomato salad

and variations

This is another case of stating what is glaringly obvious but often ignored, but a tomato salad is all about the tomatoes. All they need is a fruity olive oil and a generous seasoning of salt and black pepper. If these are not too finely ground, all the better. Fresh basil is a tomato's oldest friend and a few leaves will take the salad to sublime heights. For a few weeks in late summer we're blessed with a selection of tomatoes, organic and sun ripened. Then there are plum, beef (nasty name for a tomato), tiny red and yellow cherry, the slightly larger gardener's delight and the very cute pear-shaped, both in red and yellow. That's eight different varieties, and they look stunning on a plate. My favourite salad tomatoes are the fleshier ones with fewer seeds, thickly sliced plums and the horribly named beef, but the smaller sweet varieties add contrasts of both flavour and colour. Even two or three will double the impact of your salad, but even then the flavour is the ultimate test. The tomatoes need to be perfectly ripe but not soft, and at room temperature. I won't say there's no point in making a tomato salad with under-ripe Dutch tomatoes, but it won't raise many smiles. Salting the tomatoes before serving draws out their flavour and, in fact, about ten minutes beforehand would be ideal.

FOR FOUR:

- 800g tomatoes
- salt and pepper
- a good olive oil
- 10–12 basil leaves

DEPENDING ON THE TYPES OF TOMATO you have, either thickly slice, halve or quarter them. Put them on four plates, then sprinkle some salt and pepper and drizzle a little olive oil over them. Tear the basil leaves coarsely and scatter them over the tomatoes.

Tomato and fresh mozzarella salad

This is a classic. Go the whole hog and search out some fresh buffalo milk cheese; the cow's milk version has the texture but little flavour. Two whole fresh mozzarella cheeses, about 300–400g, will be enough for four, and could easily stretch to six or eight. Simply slice the mozzarella into as many pieces as you have hungry mouths and put one piece with each salad.

Tomato salad with rocket pesto and Knockalara sheep's cheese

Replace the mozzarella with about 40g Knockalara or other mild sheep's cheese per person, and plant a few blobs of the rocket pesto from page 37 around the plate. Leave out the basil too and replace it with a few fresh rocket leaves.

Tempura

I've been doing tempura, day in, day out, for about ten years, from five to twenty times a night, and they're all different. It is a simple dish with few ingredients and no technique required. There are some crucial conditions, but the most important is the cook's understanding of what he or she is aiming for, and the ability to make small adjustments to get it. Practice is everything. A (near) perfect tempura will have a thin, almost transparent coating of lightly browned, crisp batter, perfectly balanced in flavour with the vegetable inside. A too-thin vegetable will be smothered by the batter, while a too-thick one may not cook through or simply not taste like it's been tempura'd at all. A good tempura brings out the best in a vegetable. I've seen people rave about courgettes, for goodness sake, and a chef friend of mine once wondered what 'that brilliant orange vegetable' was - oh, a carrot! Cut the vegetables into shapes that flatter them but come naturally from themselves: carrots in long diagonals about 2-3mm thick, aubergine about the same thickness in rounds, long thin florets of broccoli and cauliflower (a broad floret head will hold water from the batter and taste raw or half-cooked), whole small shiitake mushrooms, rounds of green pepper, whole or half radishes with some stem still attached. Most vegetables tempura well, some partner each other better than others, but some that don't work well are greens like spinach and cabbage, tomatoes and other vegetables with high water content. The batter is easy to make, but only practice will help you to see exactly how much water to use. A good batter has the consistency of light pouring cream and most of it runs off the vegetable as it is lifted out, leaving a thin film of batter attached. The oil needs to be at or close to 190°C/375°F for that perfect tempura, which gives a temperature-controlled deep fryer the nod over a wok or pan of oil, but it is also crucial that the oil is clean.

Play around with combinations of vegetables. At Paradiso we've always done an eight- or nine-vegetable plate, and occasionally offered well-matched singles, duos and trios: asparagus; oyster mushroom and sweet potato; sprouting broccoli and beetroot. If you're cooking for a few people and need to do more than two batches (one might hold in an oven at a stretch), make a virtue of your predicament by serving communal batches rather than individual plates, maybe even one vegetable at a time, followed by a batch of the next vegetable and so on.

- 250g flour
- 2 egg yolks
- 380mls of cold water
- oil for deep frying
- raw vegetables, about 6–10 pieces per person

PUT THE FLOUR IN A BOWL, make a well in the centre and drop in the egg yolks, then whisk in most of the water. Add the rest if the batter isn't thin enough. Heat the oil to about (or exactly) 190°C/375°F. Drop the vegetables into the batter in batches of eight to ten. Pull them out, one at a time, with tongs or your fingers, and lower them gently into the oil. Watch them as they cook, they may need to be separated from each other or turned over. In about two minutes, the batter should have crisped evenly and you can remove that batch to a paper towel to dry.

Shoyu-ginger dip:

- 250mls shoyu
- 50mls saki or sherry
- 1 tblspn of grated ginger
- water

COMBINE THE SHOYU, saki and ginger in a jug, taste it and dilute with water as you see fit. About 100–150mls should do.

Roasted tomato soup

with summer herbs

This is our summer soup, almost the only one we serve hot for about five months. Not that summer in Ireland lasts five months, more like five days in May usually, but ripe well-flavoured tomatoes keep coming, right up to late October. It is easy to make and has a simple but intense flavour – ripe, roasted tomatoes, set off by whatever herbs you have to hand. Again, keep it simple; most of the time we use basil, oregano and parsley, no more. The passata (sieved tomatoes in a carton available in shops), is optional, depending on how well-flavoured your tomatoes were to start with. This recipe will make about 2.2 litres, enough for six to eight portions.

FOR SIX TO EIGHT:

- 2kg ripe tomatoes
- olive oil
- 8 cloves garlic
- 1 sprig of rosemary
- 1 sprig of thyme
- 2 onions
- 100mls tomato passata
- 800mls light stock or water
- seasoning
- 1 cupful of fresh herbs, coarsely chopped or torn: basil, parsley, oregano, marjoram; maybe a little of fennel, dill or chives

CHOP THE TOMATOES IN HALVES, toss them in a little olive oil and roast in a hot oven, turning occasionally, until browning. Peel the garlic cloves and add them to the tomatoes, with the rosemary and thyme, about five minutes into the cooking.

Chop the onion and cook it in a little olive oil, until soft. Transfer both the onion and the tomatoes to a large pot, discarding the herb stalks, and add in the passata and stock. Bring to the boil and simmer for about 15 minutes. Blend to get a smooth puree, then sieve it to get the skins out. If the soup is thicker than you like, you can, at this stage, dilute it with a little water and bring it back up to the boil. Season well and stir in the fresh herbs; or stir the herbs into each individual portion.

Chilled beetroot soup

with soured cream, cucumber and scallions

This soup is so beautiful to look at, as well as to eat, that I put it on summer menus despite it being one of the lowest-selling dishes ever in the history of catering. I have to confess that I don't get up frighteningly early on the occasional sunny days of summer in Ireland just to have chilled beetroot soup ready for lunch. When the first big box of fresh summer beetroot comes in I make a batch of this soup without the yoghurt and freeze small boxes of it. Be prepared, as they say. Bridget and the kids drop everything and dash to the ocean when the sun shines here, worried that it might never happen again. I take a box of frozen beetroot soup from the freezer. One important thing to remember when making chilled or frozen food is that the lower temperatures mask flavours, so you need to put in more of the flavours that you want to be prominent later.

FOR SIX TO EIGHT:

- 600g beetroot
- 2 onions
- 6 cloves of garlic
- ½ fennel bulb
- 60g potatoes
- 1 litre water
- 2 tsps dill
- 2 tsps salt
- ¼ tsp cayenne pepper
- 2 tsps balsamic vinegar
- 150mls yoghurt

FOR THE GARNISH:

- soured cream or crème fraîche
- 2 scallions, finely chopped
- very thin cucumber slices, halved

COOK THE BEETROOT IN BOILING WATER, without preparing or trimming them in any way – any knife cuts will cause colour to leak. The cooking time will depend on the size and age of the roots. The skins should come away easily by rubbing the cooked roots with your fingers under cold water.

Meanwhile chop the onions, the garlic and the fennel, and cook them in a tiny amount of oil in a soup pot. Peel and chop the potato, chop the peeled roots and add both to the pot with the water. Bring it to the boil and simmer until the potato is soft. Off the heat, add the dill, salt, cayenne pepper and vinegar, and blend to a smooth puree. Check the seasoning, remembering that chilling will dull its effect. Leave the puree to cool to room temperature before stirring in the yoghurt. The soup should be thick enough to support thin garnishes, but not cloying. If it is too thick, dilute it now or add ice cubes when you are putting it in the fridge to chill. Serve the soup in wide, shallow bowls with a blob of soured cream in the centre and an arrangement of garnishes – the scallions and cucumber slices – around the cream.

Celeriac, potato and hazelnut soup

with sautéed leeks

This is a fine autumn or winter soup, comforting and with a surprising degree of sweetness. Bridget thinks it tastes of apples. It was inspired by a lunch I wasn't even at, in Ballymaloe in East Cork. Celeriac and hazelnut soup was served and devoured, and, later, while the telling of the lunch was going on I was thinking what a brilliant combination that was. An hour later we had produced a version. I still haven't tasted the original; I don't get out enough. The weight of celeriac here, as with all measurements in this book, is a net weight, the amount that needs to go into the pot. Depending on the knobliness, size and shape of your celeriac, you might need to bring home twice or even three times that weight. Peeling them isn't so much peeling as slicing off the skin and roots. We grind the hazelnuts before they are subjected to the blending of the soup because I want them to be a flavour rather than a texture. The leeks on top add some texture as well as flavour, though you can leave them out and serve the soup with just a blob of cream or soured cream, if you like. The recipe makes two litres, enough for six to eight portions.

FOR SIX TO EIGHT:

- 2 onions
- 6 garlic cloves
- a little oil or butter
- 500g celeriac
- 150g potatoes
- 1.2 litres light stock
- 40g hazelnuts
- 1 tsp dried dill
- ¼ tsp nutmeg
- salt and pepper

FOR THE GARNISH:

- 1 medium leek
- some whipping cream

CHOP THE ONION AND GARLIC – it doesn't really matter how thickly or in what shape, everything goes under the blade of the blender later. Heat a little oil, butter or both in a large pot and start the onion and garlic cooking. Meanwhile, peel and coarsely chop the celeriac and potato and, when the onion has softened, add it to the pot with the stock. Bring this to the boil, then simmer it gently until the vegetables are all quite soft. This should take 20–30 minutes.

While the soup is simmering, roast the hazelnuts in a low – medium oven; a slow roasting is best to cook them evenly through to the centre. If you have the patience, it is best to peel the nuts now. A usually successful method is to put them in a tea-towel and rub them together. The skins will simply fall away after one or two rubbings. Any stubborn patches of skin are best ignored, they may have their reasons. Now grind the nuts as finely as possible in a food processor and stir them into the soup pot with the dill and nutmeg. Season generously with salt and pepper, then blend the soup. If it is too thick for your liking, simply add some water and remember to check the seasoning.

Trim any tough or damaged green ends off the leek, slice it in half lengthways almost to the base and wash it carefully under running water. Then chop it across into thin slices. Gently fry these in a little butter until tender, then season them and set aside. It matters little whether they are hot or at room temperature when you serve them. Put a spoon of lightly whipped cream on each serving of soup, and, on top of that, a small mound of leek.

Purple sprouting broccoli with new potatoes,

a tapenade dressing and sheep's cheese

For those of us who crave garden-fresh greenery, this broccoli is a hero, by a long way the first fresh green food to show after the long winter. From as early as February, it sprouts thin, green shoots with purple flower heads, from gangly bushes. Stems, heads, leaves, all edible, with an intense, alive, slightly peppery flavour, it needs only the briefest, simplest cooking. Steamed bundles are great with rich food or in a salad, it's brilliant with pasta and oil, and has more than enough character to take on chilli, soya sauce, sesame oil and the like in a stir fry. Within four to six weeks, it's all over as the flowers begin to seed, but by then it's all optimism in the vegetable world – everything's beginning to show and make fine promises: asparagus, spinach, spring cabbage, the beans and peas. It rarely appears in shops, so grow it or make friends with someone who does. This recipe is one I use at Paradiso to dress it up as a starter for dinner. Think of it as a warm salad and it would make a fine lunch too. The cheese is completely up to you. I would use shavings of a hard sheep's cheese like Orla or Italian pecorino, or shavings of parmesan, or crumblings of a soft sheep's cheese, like Knockalara.

FOR FOUR:

- 8 small new potatoes
- 4 handfuls of sprouting broccoli
- olive oil
- 1 small red onion, thinly sliced
- 4 dstspns tapenade (see page 35)
- about 50g sheep's cheese or parmesan

BOIL AND SLICE THE POTATOES. Trim any thick stems off the broccoli. Heat a little olive oil in a pan and toss in the broccoli and onion together. Cook over a fairly high heat, stirring all the time and occasionally splashing in a little water, for about two minutes. Now toss in the potato and cook for a few seconds to warm it a little, before tipping the lot into a bowl. Dilute the tapenade to double its volume with olive oil, stir it into the vegetables and share it out between four plates. Sprinkle some cheese shavings or crumblings over the top, or not, as you choose.

Deep-fried courgette flower parcels of sheep's cheese and pinenuts

with olive tapenade

Now and again during the summer, Organic Joe will bring us some courgettes with their flowers attached, the size of ten-year-olds' little fingers, and when the oohing and aahing is over we deep fry them, usually with a stuffing. Some parcel materials are an important part of the flavours in the dish, others are simply wrapping. Courgette flowers, for all their fragile elegance, fall into the second category, so the excitement in the dish comes from the brevity of the season when you have tiny courgettes with healthy flowers and the need to use them very soon after picking – the flowers will only be usable for a day, really. Any size of flower will do but the prettiest presentation comes from small flowers with tiny courgettes attached. If the courgette is too big, cut it off leaving a little bit attached to help hold the end of the flower together. And if you don't have sheep's cheese, pinenuts or basil, use the flowers anyway with whatever stuffing you can make, because it's one of those dishes that makes both cooks and diners feel close to nature.

FOR FOUR:

- 2 scallions
- 200g Knockalara cheese
- 2 dstspns pinenuts
- 100g breadcrumbs
- 1 egg yolk
- salt and pepper
- fresh basil leaves
- 8–12 courgette flowers, depending on their size

FOR THE BATTER:

- oil for deep frying
- 120g plain flour
- salt and pepper
- 1 egg yolk
- 300mls cold water

FOR THE TAPENADE:

- 2 tblspns tapenade (see page 35)
- 2 tblspns olive oil

CHOP THE SCALLIONS FINELY, crumble the cheese, lightly toast the pinenuts, then combine these, and mix in the crumbs and the egg yolk. Season generously but check the saltiness of the cheese first; Knockalara isn't usually salty but if you're using another sheep's cheese it may be. Chop the basil and mix it in. Gently open a courgette flower, without tearing it, and take out the stamen. Then put in some of the filling, enough to fill the flower quite firmly but leaving the darker end empty and loose – use this to close the parcel by twisting it gently. You can manipulate the filling from the outside with your fingers to make sure the flower is neatly packed and has returned to something like its former shape. Repeat with the other flowers.

Heat the oil to approximately 180°C/350°F, and meanwhile make the batter by combining the flour, salt and pepper, dropping in the egg yolk and then whisking in the water until you get a thick pouring consistency. You may not need all the water; some days you may need a little more. Place the flowers in the batter to coat them, then lower them gently into the oil. They should cook in about three or four minutes, and may need turning.

For the tapenade sauce, simply dilute the tapenade with olive oil until you have a pouring consistency you like.

To serve, place two or three parcels on each plate and drizzle some tapenade around each.

Roasted pepper, olive and brie tartlets

with a balsamic vinaigrette

These are very simple tarts, with just a few well-met flavours layered together, and no eggs or custard in sight. They make a classy, elegant starter and are very easy to put together. I would never make such a tiny amount of either the pastry or the pepper puree. If you at least double both, you could be turning these out for days, or for many more people, and you will find many other uses for them too. The sauce, or vinaigrette as it likes to be called, makes enough for more than ten, but it would be hard to get a smaller volume to come together and it keeps well.

FOR FOUR:

- pastry from 80g flour as on page 110
- 1 red pepper, roasted and peeled
- 1 garlic clove, chopped
- 1 tblspn olive oil
- 1 yellow pepper, roasted and peeled
- 12 black olives, stoned and quartered
- 80g brie

ROLL THE PASTRY to fit four shallow tartlet cases, and blind bake them as described on page 110.

Chop the peeled red pepper and put it in a small pan with the garlic, olive oil and enough water to cover. Bring this to the boil and cook at a lively simmer until the water has almost evaporated, then puree what's left and leave it to cool. You should now have a thick, intensely flavoured spread.

Chop the yellow pepper into dice of about 1cm and mix them with the chopped olives

To put the tarts together, put some pepper puree in each, maybe two teaspoons or so, then a generous tablespoon of the yellow pepper and olives on top of that, and finally some thinly sliced brie. Bake at 375°F (Gas Mark 5) until the brie melts – about six to eight minutes.

Serve one tartlet per person with a thin drizzle of the balsamic vinaigrette poured around it.

FOR THE BALSAMIC VINAIGRETTE:

- 250mls olive oil
- 1 clove of garlic, crushed
- 120mls tomato passata
- 80mls balsamic vinegar
- salt and pepper

FOR THE BALSAMIC VINAIGRETTE, put all of the ingredients in a jug and use a hand liquidiser to blend the sauce to an emulsified, thickened consistency. Check the flavour – you may need to adjust one or all of the components. If the sauce subsequently separates, just blend it back together again before serving. There is enough here for at least ten portions and it will keep for a week or so in the fridge.

Beetroot mousse

with orange and fennel scented yoghurt

Generally, I don't like 'soft' food, soufflés and such fripperies, so why I decided to turn a fine hard root into a light sponge I honestly can't remember. I suppose the appeal of mousses is that the dish becomes almost totally focused on taste, so for beetroot lovers this is a perfect way to bask in its flavour, better even than a thick soup. In truth, I don't sell many of these, but it does have devoted fans, people who get calls in the middle of the night when it makes an appearance. The scented yoghurt is a natural companion for beetroot, in the way that a beetroot soup would have a dollop of yoghurt or soured cream on top. Use a thick, rich, unsweetened yoghurt. The quantities below should fill six large ramekins of about 150mls each.

TO MAKE SIX SERVINGS:

- 400g beetroot
- 2 cloves of garlic
- juice of ½ lemon
- 120g cream cheese
- 2 eggs
- 2 egg whites
- 40mls cream
- large pinch of cayenne pepper
- large pinch of nutmeg
- ¼ tsp salt

BOIL THE BEETROOT in plenty of water until a knife will pass easily through it. This can take from half an hour to two hours, depending on the age and size of the roots. The skin should come away easily when rubbed with your fingers under cold water.

When the beetroot has cooled, chop it and place in a food processor with the garlic, lemon juice and cream cheese, and blend to a smooth puree. With the motor running, add in the eggs, then the egg whites. The cream needs only to be stirred or pulsed in, using it to dilute the puree to the consistency you want. This should be a very thick pouring consistency, but not so thick that it needs spooning rather than pouring. Add the seasonings at the end.

Preheat the oven to 350°F (Gas Mark 4). Oil the ramekins, and place a piece of greaseproof paper in the bottom of each. Fill the ramekins almost to the top, place them in an oven dish into which pour boiling water up to halfway, and cook until the mousses are firm to the touch. This should take about 50–60 minutes. Leave them to cool for at least 10 minutes before turning them out – they can be served immediately or allowed to cool to room temperature. They can even be chilled and carefully reheated back up to 'warm'. Serve one mousse per person with a little pool of orange scented yoghurt.

FOR THE YOGHURT:

- 1 tsp fennel seeds
- 1 orange
- 100mls water
- 250mls yoghurt
- ¼ tsp salt
- pinch of cayenne pepper

TOAST THE FENNEL SEEDS LIGHTLY in a heavy pan, then finely grind them. Peel the orange in strips, and put the rind in a saucepan with the juice of half the orange, the fennel seeds, and the water. Bring to the boil and simmer until the liquid is reduced to about 50mls. Strain off the solids (most of the fennel will get through) and stir the liquid into the yoghurt. Season and check the consistency – it should be a thick pouring cream.

Pan-fried parmesan-stuffed artichoke fritters

with basil aioli

To be honest, there's no better way to eat artichokes than leaf by leaf in the classic way, with a vinaigrette or mayonnaise dip and the promise of the heart coming closer as you nibble. Somehow, people don't seem to feel like spending half the evening doing that anymore. This recipe came out of an artichoke glut. We got a few boxes of organic artichokes at 'a good price' and I realised we'd never sell them fast enough served one at a time in the traditional way. So we stuffed them with parmesan, paired them with a basil dip, and they disappeared in no time. How many artichokes you prepare depends on their size, how many you've got and how much work you're prepared to do. Two each is fine, three very extravagant, and you wouldn't be ashamed of serving one large one per person with some leaves and the aioli.

FOR FOUR:

- 8–12 artichokes
- lemon juice
- 50g parmesan, grated
- 150g breadcrumbs
- 2 eggs
- 100mls milk
- 50g flour
- some mixed salad leaves, equivalent to one small head of lettuce

FOR THE BASIL AIOLI:

- 1 egg
- 4 cloves garlic
- 250mls basil oil
- salt and black pepper
- lemon juice (optional)

MAKE THE AIOLI FIRST. (This is a simple version. On page 40 there is a roasted garlic-rosemary aioli recipe with detailed instructions.) Beat the egg and garlic in a food processor for a minute or so, until the egg is frothy and the garlic crushed. With the motor running, slowly pour in the basil oil until you have a thick emulsion. Season with salt and pepper, and add a little lemon juice if you like.

Trim the leaves from the artichokes and remove the hairy choke, rubbing lemon juice to the artichoke heart as it becomes exposed, to prevent discolouring. Boil the artichokes for 10–20 minutes until they are just tender.

To make the filling for the artichokes, put the parmesan and 50g of the breadcrumbs into a food processor and blend them for a minute or so, then add one egg and blend again to get a thick paste. Use this paste to fill the cavities in the artichokes.

Coat the filled artichokes in the remaining breadcrumbs. To do this, first whisk the second egg and the milk together. Dip the artichokes in flour, dunk them in the egg and milk, then toss them in the breadcrumbs until fully coated.

Heat about a quarter inch of oil in a frying pan to a moderate heat, and fry the artichokes, turning them once to brown both sides. Keep them warm in an oven while you fry a second batch if necessary.

Serve two or three artichokes per person, with some salad leaves and a little bowl of the aioli on the side for dipping.

Oyster mushroom and smoked Gubeen ravioli with sage and paprika butter

Gubeen is a semi-soft cheese made in West Cork. It makes a perfect partner for oyster mushrooms because it is so delicately smoked. Don't substitute a cheese with a strong smoky flavour. This quantity should make enough for twelve giant ravioli, 8cm square, and at two parcels each, is a generous starter. Feel free to make more, smaller, ravioli if you prefer. We use thin sheets of spinach pasta for this, purely for the colour contrast with the red-orange butter. We've also been blessed with a secret supply of Spanish paprika, with distinctly sweet and slightly smoky flavours, which has changed my attitude to paprika – previously I thought it to be a powdery dye.

FOR SIX:

- 1 onion, finely chopped
- 3 garlic cloves, crushed
- tblspn butter
- 400g oyster mushrooms, diced
- 2 tblspns white wine
- 60g breadcrumbs
- 1 egg yolk
- 60g smoked Gubeen, in tiny dice
- parsley
- salt and pepper
- 2 fresh pasta sheets, 16cm x 48cm or equivalent

FOR THE BUTTER:

- 225g butter
- fresh sage
- paprika

START THE ONION AND GARLIC in a tablespoon of butter, add the mushrooms after a couple of minutes, turn up the heat and cook for one minute before pouring in the wine. Cook until the mushrooms are done and the liquid evaporated. This should only take two or three minutes. Tip the mushrooms into a bowl and leave to cool before adding the crumbs, egg yolk, smoked Gubeen cheese, some parsley and seasoning.

Meanwhile, make the butter. It is difficult to give specific quantities here and best to make too much as it keeps well in the fridge. If you like sage you're sure to find another use for it. Soften some butter with a fork, say a 225g block, or half of one, and stir into it some finely chopped sage and enough paprika to give it a definite red-orange colour. The butter needs to be at room temperature when used or it will just sit there on top of the pasta instead of melting. Don't heat it, however, melted butter is a different animal altogether.

Cut the pasta into twenty-four 8cm squares and place a small mound of mushrooms on twelve of them. Brush the exposed pasta with water, place another square on top of each and press the edges together, trying to remove any air pockets at the same time. Do this one at a time or the water will just soak into the pasta as it waits for you to get around to it. You can store these on baking parchment, lightly floured and clingfilmed or even frozen. We usually part cook them before storing, lightly oiled, on parchment, but that's catering for you. Either way, to cook the ravioli, drop them into boiling water, make sure they don't stick to each other or the pan, and check them often. They should cook in three to five minutes, but that depends on the thickness and freshness of the pasta, among other things. Testing is the only way to know. Make sure the six plates are warm, slide a couple of ravioli on to each and daub a few small lumps of butter over them.

Braised spinach parcels of feta, green pepper and caramelized onion

with a sweet-spiced beetroot cream

This is almost worth making for the colours alone. Luckily, it tastes good too. There's a lot going on inside the parcels, the tangy crunch of the almost-raw pepper mingling with the sweet, soft onions, all dominated by the feta. Real sheep's milk feta is best, but the cheap Danish stuff works well too, if I may be excused for saying it. Be careful with the measurements for the spices in the beetroot cream. It might be best to start with less and add in a little more at the end – the beetroot itself should be the main flavour.

FOR FOUR:

- 120g onions
- 1 tsp butter
- 1 tsp olive oil
- ½ tsp cumin seeds
- 1 tsp light musovado sugar
- 1 tsp balsamic vinegar
- rind of ½ lemon
- ½ green pepper, finely diced
- 30g breadcrumbs
- 50g feta, crumbled
- pinch of cayenne pepper
- 3–4 leaves of fresh mint

- 12 good-sized spinach leaves

FOR THE BEETROOT CREAM:

- 100g beetroot, cooked & peeled
- 200mls water
- ¼ tsp cinnamon
- ½ tsp nutmeg
- ¼ tsp ground ginger
- 2 cloves
- 1 star anise
- pinch of cayenne pepper
- 100mls cream
- salt

SLICE THE ONIONS into fairly thin quarter rounds and put them in a heavy pan with the butter, olive oil and cumin seeds. Stew them gently for twenty to thirty minutes, stirring occasionally to prevent sticking or browning. The onion should be softened and beginning to caramelize. Put in the sugar, vinegar and lemon juice and cook for a few minutes more until the liquids become syrupy. The green pepper needs to be cooked a little, so I add it to the onion pan for the last minute, but if you're unsure of the timing, cook it separately for a minute and add it off the heat. Allow the onion and pepper to cool before stirring in the breadcrumbs and crumbled feta, with a pinch of cayenne and a few chopped leaves of fresh mint – three or four will do, you don't want mint to be a dominant flavour here.

Dunk the spinach leaves in boiling water for a few seconds, literally in and out, then into cold water immediately to cool. Lay them flat on a worktop and place a small amount of the filling near the base of each, one to two teaspoons, depending on the size of the leaf. Manipulate the filling into a low rectangular shape, fold the sides of the leaf over the filling, then roll the leaf up to get a neat parcel. Chop the beetroot into small pieces and put it in a pan with the water and the spices. Bring it to the boil, simmer it very gently for ten minutes or so, then remove the anise and the cloves, and blend the rest to a very fine puree. It should have the consistency of thick pouring cream. Put this puree back in the pan, add the cream and bring it to the boil for a few seconds only. Any prolonged boiling at this stage will cause the beautiful colour to fade to pale pink with hints of brown! If you use this sauce for something else, you may want to leave it thinner, but our experience has been that the spinach parcels pick up very little of a thin sauce, so it becomes a merely pretty colour on the plate. Put the sauce through a sieve and return it to the pan to be warmed through.

To cook the parcels, heat about a quarter inch of water in a wide frying pan, adding two tablespoons of olive oil to the water. Gently place some parcels in the water and cook them gently for eight to ten minutes, basting them occasionally. Ideally, the water should be almost all evaporated and the parcels will have taken on some of the oil. Keep some warm in a low oven (don't bake the poor, sensitive things) while you do a second batch. Serve three in a pile on a plate with the warm beetroot cream poured around them.

Aubergine sticky rice rolls

with a sesame-soya sauce dip and wasabi

This is based on the recipe for sushi rice which we've been making ever since Paradiso opened. There are hundreds of recipes for, and lectures on, the art of sushi making so I'm giving you this variation instead. The rolls can be served at room temperature or as we serve them, warmed up a few degrees, though not hot. Offer them on individual plates or communally, or as part of a selection with tempura, pickles, maybe some sushi, fried cabbage or a seaweed salad.

FOR FOUR:

- 500g sushi, pudding or pearl rice
- 600mls cold water
- 100mls coconut milk
- 2 tblspns white wine, rice vinegar or lemon juice
- 3 aubergines
- shoyu-ginger dip (see page 57)
- toasted sesame oil
- wasabi powder

RINSE THE RICE A COUPLE OF TIMES to take out some of the starch, then put it in a pan with the cold water, bring it to the boil and simmer over a low heat, covered, for exactly ten minutes. Turn the heat off but leave the pan for a further ten minutes. Now tip the rice into a bowl and sift it with a slotted spoon as you add the coconut milk and the vinegar. Set the rice aside to cool for an hour or so.

Trim the aubergine by cutting two thin slices off opposite sides lengthways, then slice the rest of the aubergine lengthways into long, fairly thin sheets, getting about six from an average aubergine. Brush both sides of each piece with oil and roast them in a hot oven, 340–350°F (Gas Mark 4), until cooked through (about ten minutes). When both the rice and aubergine have cooled to room temperature, take some rice and shape a thin layer of it on an aubergine slice, leaving an inch of uncovered aubergine at the end. Use a little pressure to keep the rice together and even, but not so much that you push it through the aubergine. Now, roll up the aubergine, again applying some pressure to make a tight roll and keep the sides tidy. Repeat with the other aubergine slices.

The dip is simply the shoyu-ginger dip on page 57 with a few drops of toasted sesame oil stirred in just before serving. Prepare the wasabi by stirring cold water into the powder to get a thick mustard-like paste.

Corn pancakes of roasted pepper, red onion and goats' cheese

with a fennel-chilli salsa

These little pancake parcels are packed with a very familiar taste combination – corn, peppers and goats' cheese. They are great as starters, main courses, snacks and anything you fancy, and are simple to make, except for one thing – sometimes the batter sticks to the pan for no obvious reason. Honestly, it just happens, sometimes halfway through frying what seems like a perfectly well-behaved batch. You curse a little, try again, then throw the lot out. So make a double amount of the batter, and please send any thoughts you have on the matter to the editor. Anyway, I've just checked the recipe below and it worked like a dream. The saffron and paprika are in there purely to boost the colour of the cornmeal. We always serve these with the fennel-chilli salsa on page 33, but pestos, simple tomato sauces or even cream-herb sauces would be fine too. During the long leek season, I always replace the red onions with leeks – one average-sized leek would do here.

TO MAKE FOUR TO FIVE PANCAKES, 20cm IN DIAMETER:

- a few strands of saffron
- 25g plain flour
- 50g fine cornmeal
- ¼ tsp salt
- pinch of cayenne pepper
- ¼ tsp paprika
- 1 egg
- 150mls milk

SOAK THE SAFFRON in a small amount of boiling water for 5–10 minutes. Sift the flour and cornmeal, salt and peppers. Beat the egg and milk together briefly, then whisk this into the flour and cornmeal, to get a smooth batter. Add the saffron and check that the batter has a fairly thin pouring consistency. Leave to sit while you warm a 20cm crêpe pan, then fry the pancakes in olive oil. Stir the batter well before each pouring, as the corn tends to sink in the batter. This should make four pancakes, about half as thick again as delicate crêpes, out of which you can make twelve parcels, enough for six starters or four main courses. Nevertheless, I would still make a double batter.

FOR THE FILLING (TWELVE PARCELS):

- 3 red peppers
- 2 red onions
- 3 cloves of garlic
- a little olive oil
- 160g goats' cheese, crumbly log type
- 80g breadcrumbs
- seasoning
- fennel-chilli salsa (see page 33)

ROAST AND PEEL THE PEPPERS, as on page 19. Chop into small dice. Chop the onion and garlic and cook them in a little olive oil for a few minutes. Add the peppers and cook for a minute, then transfer the lot to a bowl. Wait for it to cool before adding the rest of the ingredients, crumbling the cheese to pieces roughly similar in size to the pepper dice.

To fill the pancakes, first cut the pancakes into three parts (large pie-wedge style). Place a generous amount of filling down the centre of each piece, then fold over, first, one side, then the other, manipulating the filling to get an evenly filled triangular package. Place the parcels seam side down on baking parchment on an oven tray, brush with olive oil and bake at a moderate heat, 350–375°F (Gas Mark 4–5) for about ten minutes, until warmed through and lightly crisped. Serve two per person with a generous dollop of the fennel-chilli salsa.

Carrot, almond and feta terrine,

in vine leaves, with a green pepper-coriander salsa

This quantity makes a terrine to fill one 2lb loaf tin and that should give you enough for eight to ten first courses. And a palate-tingling starter it is too, with the sweetness of the carrots, almonds and vine leaves set off by the salty tang of the feta. The salsa we serve with it adds its own dimensions of texture, sharpness and the heady scent of fresh coriander. Don't wait for someone's birthday to try it though; the terrine has enough texture, richness and flavour to be a meal in itself. We serve it for lunch with the salsa and a couscous or potato dish. You'll also get four to five generous main courses from this quantity.

FOR EIGHT TO TEN STARTERS:

- 500g carrots
- 1 tblspn butter
- 1 tsp cumin seeds
- 6 garlic cloves, chopped
- 1 leek, washed and finely chopped
- a little olive oil
- 80g whole almonds, lightly toasted
- 100g cream cheese
- 2 eggs
- salt
- pinch of cayenne pepper
- 1 tsp dill
- 1 pack of vine leaves
- 100g feta

CHOP THE CARROTS INTO SMALL PIECES, and stew them, covered, in a heavy pan, with the butter, cumin and garlic. They may need an occasional splash of water to prevent them sticking, but they often manage without it and come out tender and juicy in about 20 minutes. Meanwhile, chop the leek finely and cook it in a little olive oil for just a minute or so. In a food processor, chop the almonds, then put them in a bowl. Now chop the cooked carrots in the processor until they become a coarse mash. Take out half, add in the cream cheese and eggs and blend until you get a smooth puree this time. Stir this into the almonds with the carrot mash, the cooked leeks, salt, cayenne and dill.

Preheat the oven to 350°F (Gas Mark 4). Brush a 2lb loaf tin with olive oil and use the vine leaves to line it, making sure that they overlap each other well, and that you have a good deal of overhanging leaves. It's better if you're closer to a double layer of leaves than a single. Try to apply some olive oil anywhere that leaves are overlapping each other. Put half of the carrot filling into the tin, scatter crumbled feta over this, then spoon in the rest of the carrot. Lay some more vine leaves on top and fold over the overhanging leaves. Put a light weight on top (I use baking parchment and dried chickpeas) and put the tin in an oven dish. Pour boiling water into the dish to halfway up the tin, and cook the terrine in the preheated oven for 50–60 minutes. The top of the terrine will feel firm and slightly risen when it's done. Leave the terrine to cool for 10–15 minutes before turning it out on to a plate. Use a very sharp knife to cut slices and serve it warm with the green pepper and coriander salsa on page 32.

Peperonata with olive-grilled ciabatta,

basil and parmesan shavings

The quality of the oil is crucial here, and the quantity too, though I know it seems a lot and there are many peperonata recipes without it - I once ate one in Sicily that was close to a puree. The idea of my version is a very rich stew, meltingly comforting but with a little kick, the sweetness of the peppers drawn out by slow and low simmering in a fruity olive oil: the slowness teases out the peppers, the low heat leaves the flavour in the olive oil. You can leave out the olives and the chilli, but cook something else rather than leave out the oil. This is my favourite way of serving peperonata, though grilled polenta shows it off well too, and it's not too proud to act as a side dish, especially if eggs, risotto or pasta are involved.

FOR SIX:

- 1 onion
- 6 garlic cloves, peeled and halved
- 100mls olive oil
- 6 red and/or yellow peppers
- 1 small chilli, finely chopped
- 3 tomatoes, sliced in half rounds
- 10 black olives, stoned
- salt
- 1 small ciabatta loaf
- 3 tblspns tapenade (see page 35)
- fresh basil
- 60g fresh parmesan

SLICE THE ONION INTO THIN QUARTER ROUNDS, put it in a heavy pan with the garlic and the olive oil and slowly bring the oil up to a very low heat. Chop the peppers into thickish strips, about 15mm, and add them to the pan with the chilli. Bring the heat back up to a low simmer and cover the pan. Check occasionally to make sure that the contents are not just sitting there, but stewing away gently. When the peppers are just tender, stir in the sliced tomatoes and the olives, and cook on until the peppers are beginning to soften and the tomatoes to break down. Add salt and turn off the heat, but leave the lid on, while you do the ciabatta. Like a lot of rich Mediterranean food, the peperonata will benefit from sitting quietly for a while and cooling down a few degrees.

Cut the ciabatta in half lengthways, spread a thin layer of tapenade on both halves and drizzle some olive oil over this. Pop the bread into a hot oven for a few minutes, or under a hot grill.

Serve the peperonata and some ciabatta wedges with plenty of freshly torn basil and shavings of parmesan scattered over.

Asparagus and Gabriel cheese gratin

I like asparagus roasted, grilled, warm in salads or dunked in mayonnaise, and all the other ways it likes to be done, but this is my favourite asparagus dish and the first one I reach for when the season starts. There are strong flavours here, so balance is important, which is why I like to do each plate separately. Too much of the cream sauce can drown the asparagus, too much of the crumble will spoil the texture as well as the flavour, and even the balance in the crumble is variable. Gabriel is a hard cheese with a tangy, peppery taste, mild when it's young but intensifying as it ages, so the amount you need can vary. The perfect gratin will have just enough sauce to be absorbed by the asparagus and the crumble, which is scattered loosely, but generously, over the plate. If you see someone scooping it up with their finger or licking the plate, you've miscalculated, but obviously not too badly.

FOR FOUR:

- 16–20 asparagus spears
- 1 onion, quartered
- 4 whole garlic cloves
- 80mls white wine
- 150mls cream
- 1 tsp strong prepared mustard
- salt and pepper
- 60g breadcrumbs
- 40g Gabriel cheese
- 1 dstspn butter

SNAP THE TOUGH ENDS OFF THE ASPARAGUS, wash them and save them. Cook the asparagus tips in boiling water for a few minutes – they should be just short of tender – then cool them. Now put the ends into a pot with the onion and garlic, the wine and about 300mls of the asparagus water. Bring it to the boil and keep at a lively simmer for about 15 minutes. Strain off the vegetables and return the stock to the pan. You should have 150mls left at most; if there is more, simply boil it for a few minutes more to reduce the volume. Then pour in the cream and mustard, and cook the sauce at a rolling boil until you have about 200mls of a fairly thick pouring sauce. Season cautiously with salt and pepper.

Make a crumble by combining the crumbs and cheese and stirring in the butter, which should be softened almost to the point of melting, and some seasoning. Now you have two choices, depending on your facilities and ambitions: (a) arrange the asparagus in an oven dish with the cream poured over, sprinkle a generous but not blanketing amount of the crumble over that, and place the dish under a hot grill until the crumble browns and the cheese begins to melt; or (b) arrange individual portions on plates and grill. I prefer the second, it only takes a minute for each plate and gives you much more control over the amount of sauce on each portion.

Three wontons in a ginger broth

This dish is almost all John Healy's, a Café Paradiso cook, and a man who likes his food delicately flavoured and calmly composed to look at. We serve three tiny wontons in a shallow bowl of broth with a few carefully cut and placed garnishes. It would seem a much more straightforward dish if it was simply one type of wonton and the broth, and that might be the best way to do it the first time. But the beauty of it is in the three different shapes and flavours and how they interact with the subtle broth. Make the fillings in advance or while the stock is simmering. The quantities are tiny but two of them are very simple to make and the third, cabbage and tofu, just has a few more ingredients. Both the broth recipe and the three fillings together make enough for eight to ten portions if you allow one of each wonton per person as a delicate starter. Two of each won't kill anyone's appetite, but don't crowd the bowl or the dish will lose its elegance. And if it is to feed people, rather than to titillate them, four people would have little trouble scoffing the lot.

FOR THE BROTH:

- 1.2 litres water
- 60g ginger, chopped or sliced
- 4 cloves of garlic, peeled
- 1 onion, chopped
- ½ fennel bulb, chopped
- 1 hot chilli, whole
- a handful of parsley stalk
- a handful of coriander stalk
- 1 tblspn shoyu
- 1 tblspn sherry
- 1 tsp salt

TO FILL TEN WONTONS:

- 100g savoy or spring cabbage
- 1 small onion, finely chopped
- 2 garlic cloves, finely chopped
- 1 tsp coriander seeds, ground
- 1 tsp green peppercorns, ground
- 80g tofu, crumbled
- 50mls coconut milk
- 2 tsp ground almonds
- 1 pack of small wonton wrappers, 5cm square
- 2 tsps shoyu

TO FILL TEN WONTONS:

- 100g oyster mushrooms
- 1 tsp grated ginger
- large pinch of salt

PUT THE WATER IN A LARGE POT with the ginger, garlic cloves, onion, fennel, chilli and the herb stalks. Bring it just to the boil, cover it and leave it on a very low heat for an hour or so. Strain the stock through a sieve and return the liquid to the pot – you should still have a litre or so of broth left. Add the shoyu, sherry and salt and, just before you cook the wontons, bring the broth back up to a low simmer.

Shred the cabbage into very thin strips, about 2cm long and fry it with the onion and spices in a wok until the cabbage wilts and softens a little. Add the tofu and coconut and cook over high heat until the liquid has all but evaporated. Off the heat, stir in the almonds and leave to cool in a bowl.

Chop the mushrooms very finely and fry them briefly in a little oil with the ginger and salt. Leave to cook.

Boil or steam the pumpkin, then mash it. Finely chop the spring onion and chilli and cook them briefly in a little oil, then stir them into the pumpkin with the salt and coriander.

Lay a few wonton wrappers on a worktop and dampen the edges with water. Place a small amount of one filling near the base, fold in the sides and roll up the wrapper to form a parcel. Do a few at a time and keep the remaining wrappers covered to stop them drying out. Store the finished wontons on lightly floured baking parchment. Wrap the other fillings in different shapes so you can distinguish them later. A pouch-shape is good, with the filling placed in the centre and the four corners pulled up and pinched together to form a neck. Or sweet-wrapper style, with the two sides twisted to seal in the filling.

TO FILL TEN WONTONS:

- 100g pumpkin
- 1 spring onion
- 1 small hot Thai chilli
- large pinch of salt
- a little fresh coriander

Prepare two or three thinly sliced vegetables as garnishes before you cook the wantons. Reheat the broth. Place the wontons into it and simmer for two to three minutes, then transfer one or two of each to the waiting bowls and ladle some broth over each. Place some of your garnishes into each bowl or serve separately at the table. If you are cooking a lot of wontons, it might be an idea to use a second pot to avoid overcrowding.

Leek and pinenut timbale

with a tomato, coriander and puy lentil concasse

What with the pinenuts and the chunky concasse sauce, this timbale has more texture than the average savoury pudding. Leeks and ginger are excellent together and they interact beautifully with the coriander in the concasse. You will need six ramekins of about 150mls capacity, though any vessel will do – I have successfully used cups and small bowls.

FOR SIX:

- 500g leeks, washed and finely chopped
- a little olive oil
- 4 cloves garlic, crushed
- 1 dstspn grated ginger
- ¼ tsp cayenne pepper
- ½ tsp salt
- juice half a lime
- 80g pinenuts, lightly toasted
- 2 eggs
- 150g cream cheese
- 2 egg whites
- 150mls cream

STEW THE LEEKS IN A LITTLE OLIVE OIL, with the garlic and ginger, until just tender. Stir in the seasonings, lime and pinenuts, and remove from the heat. Meanwhile, make a custard by beating the eggs and cream cheese together in a food processor, then adding the egg whites, and finally the cream. Add the custard to the leeks when they have cooked a little.

Preheat an oven to 375°F (Gas Mark 5). Brush individual pudding bowls or ramekins with olive oil, place a piece of parchment or greaseproof paper in the bottom of each, and fill them almost to the top with the timbale mixture. Place the bowls in an oven dish, pour in boiling water to at least halfway up the ramekins, and put the dish in the oven. Cook the timbales for 40–60 minutes, until they are just set. Leave the timbales to stand for 5–10 minutes before turning them out. Run a table knife around between each timbale and its ramekin, upturn it on to a plate and pat the end to make sure it has loosened on to the plate.

Surround each timbale with a tablespoon or two of the concasse, which can be either at room temperature or heated through very briefly.

FOR THE CONCASSE:

- approx. 120mls olive oil
- 3 tomatoes
- 1 tblspn chopped fresh coriander
- 2 tblspns cooked puy lentils
- salt to taste

DESEED THE TOMATOES and chop them into small dice. Stir in all the other ingredients, using just enough olive oil to give a moist consistency. Simply stir everything together shortly before serving.

Deep-fried salsify and celeriac fritters

with a blue cheese cream

Salsify is difficult to grow well and messy to work with, but its earthy, vaguely nutty, flavour can give subtle pleasures other roots don't even contemplate. The trouble is in the peeling – it is awkward and messy. Celeriac has a much more up-front flavour; like that of celery, would you believe? I combine the two partly because I like the flavours and the shapes together, and partly because preparing the volume required for the restaurant from salsify alone would be a chore too far. I once read a menu from a famous and huge London restaurant that offered salsify as a side order, and my heart went out to the poor lad with the peeler in the back corner of the kitchen. Because these fritters look so simple, I recommend you find a way to make sure your guests know how much trouble you went to. For the blue cheese cream, as with all cooked blue cheese dishes, it is best to use a mature, strong cheese – a little goes a long way.

FOR FOUR:

- 400g salsify, after peeling
- juice of a lemon
- 400g celeriac, after peeling
- 2 eggs
- 200mls milk
- plain flour
- approx. 200g breadcrumbs, with a little dill and seasoning added

FOR THE BLUE CHEESE CREAM:

- 50mls white wine
- 50mls light stock
- 2 whole cloves garlic, peeled
- 1 small onion, halved (or 2 shallots)
- 200mls cream
- 80–100g strong blue cheese, such as stilton, gorgonzola or a mature Irish one
- pinch of ground nutmeg and cayenne pepper
- small bunch of fresh chives, chopped

PEEL THE SALSIFY OVER NEWSPAPER or a wide tray and, to avoid discolouration, as you peel drop it into water to which you have added the juice of a lemon. Cut the peeled roots into pieces about 6–10cm long. Any very thick pieces should also be cut in half lengthways. Drop into boiling water and cook until tender (about eight to ten minutes).

The celeriac also needs to be peeled, but it doesn't discolour anything like as fast and the peeling is best done with a knife, more like slicing the skin off, really. Chop it into two-bite pieces about 1cm thick and of random shape, and boil these until just tender (about six to eight minutes).

Whisk together the eggs and milk, then set up a short assembly line: coat the vegetables first in flour, then the egg mix, and finally the breadcrumbs. Deep fry the fritters at about 170°C/325–350°F until crisp and lightly browned. Do them in batches and keep them warm in the oven while you do the rest.

Put the wine, stock, garlic, onion and cream in a pan and boil them for five minutes until the volume has reduced by half, then crumble the cheese into the sauce and leave it on very low heat until the cheese has melted. (Don't cook the cheese, just let it melt.) Now take out the garlic and onion, add in a pinch each of nutmeg and cayenne pepper, and some chives. Check the taste to make sure there is as much 'blue' flavour as you want. Leave the sauce to cool almost to room temperature, when it is thicker and the flavours clearer, though you can use it warmer if you prefer.

To serve, simply arrange a jumble of fritters on each plate, and pour a generous stream of cream around them.

Oyster mushrooms

pan-fried in gingered butter with wasabi mash

I have to admit that I'm not a lover of dense, earthy mushrooms, which is why I'm always delighted to get a delivery of these beautiful, delicate oyster mushrooms. Their subtle flavour copes with ginger brilliantly. Mind you, some of the oyster mushrooms for sale in supermarkets have no more flavour than their packaging and can't cope with anything. Very fresh, pink-gilled field mushrooms would be a good substitute or, similarly, fresh shiitakes. We add the gingered butter at the end to leave the ginger flavour clean and fresh, and so that the butter can act as a sauce on the plate. You will need only half or less of the wasabi mash recipe on page 23, a tablespoon each is enough to work as a foil for the mushrooms.

FOR FOUR:

- wasabi mash, (see page 23)
- 50g butter
- 1 tblspn grated ginger
- 300–400g fresh oyster mushrooms

MAKE THE MASH FIRST as frying the mushrooms only takes a couple of minutes. Soften half of the butter and stir the ginger into it. Trim any tough stalks from the mushrooms. Tear large mushrooms into two or three pieces, leave smaller ones whole. Slowly melt the rest of the butter in a wide shallow pan. Just as it begins to froth, put in the mushrooms, turn up the heat a little and cook the mushrooms at a gently sizzling fry, turning them now and then and generally giving them plenty of attention. Oyster mushrooms don't leak juices like other mushrooms, so if they're not cooking in the butter they're not cooking. Add a generous sprinkling of salt in the early stages of the cooking to help tease out the little juice they do have. They will shrink and colour a little as they cook, and should be done in three to five minutes. Use a knife or fork to check their tenderness, then put in the gingered butter, stir it once and take the pan off the heat immediately.

Put small mounds of wasabi mash on plates and surround this with the mushrooms. Spoon every last drop of the buttery pan juices over the mushrooms.

Gingered sweet potato spring roll

with sesame-fried cabbage and a coconut-chilli cream

We were making and selling these like proverbial hot cakes for a few weeks when I accidentally brought back some rice flour pastry sheets from the market. They were dried and had to be moistened all over before use (we didn't get that information from the pack, which, clearly, was never meant to be exported). This doubled the messiness of the job, and the time spent on it, something for which I wasn't thanked. But everyone agreed that they were worth it, so we stuck with them, until the supply ran out. Wheatflour pastry works very well too, but try to buy a brand that has only flour, water and salt in the ingredients. Using egg white to seal the rolls instead of water, or a paste made from water and cornflour, will give you an added sense of security, especially if you choose to deep fry instead of a gentler shallow fry. We usually serve one of these as a starter on a dinner menu, though a bigger portion makes a great lunch. The quantities here are for eight spring rolls, enough for eight starters or four main courses.

FOR EIGHT ROLLS:

- 1 large onion, quartered and thinly sliced
- 4 garlic cloves, chopped
- 2 tsps grated ginger
- 1 small Thai chilli, chopped or ground
- 1 tsp coriander seeds, ground
- 400g sweet potato
- 2 tsps lemon juice
- 2 tsps shoyu
- 1 tblspn chopped fresh coriander
- 8 spring roll pastry sheets

FRY THE ONION WITH THE SPICES in a little cooking oil, until the onion softens. Meanwhile, peel the sweet potatoes and chop them into pieces about the length of matchsticks but twice as fat. Cook these in boiling water for two minutes until almost tender, drain them and transfer to the onion pan with the lemon, shoyu and fresh coriander. Cook for a few minutes more to fully soften the potato – it should become a little starchy and partly break up. Leave this to cool before filling the pastries.

Lay a sheet of pastry on a worktop, facing you as a diamond shape. Spread a hefty tablespoonful of the filling about two inches up from the base and about three inches long, then brush the edges of the pastry with water. Roll up the pastry one full turn before folding in the sides, then continue rolling all the way up. Repeat with the other pastry sheets.

In a frying pan, heat enough oil to come halfway up the spring rolls. Cook the rolls over a medium heat, turning them once or twice, until lightly browned and crisp. Drain the pastries on paper before serving them with a little pile of sesame-fried cabbage (see page 29) and some coconut-chilli cream and serve.

FOR THE COCONUT-CHILLI CREAM:

- 200mls soured cream or yoghurt
- 2–4 tsps sambal oelek
- a little chopped fresh coriander
- 200mls coconut milk

THE QUANTITIES FOR THIS VERY SIMPLE, brilliant, multi-purpose sauce are difficult to dictate. Basically, I would take a container (or half of one) of soured cream or yoghurt, stir in some sambal and lots of chopped fresh coriander, dilute with coconut milk to get a thick pouring consistency, and then check the chilli level – add either more sambal or soured cream to adjust it.

Mains

Roasted vegetable ratatouille and grilled ciabatta ¶ Herbed potato tortilla ¶ Squash, butterbean and leek stew ¶ Wild rice and parsnip fritters ¶ Mushroom, pak choy and eggroll stir fry ¶ Noodles, tofu, leeks and greens ¶ Baked leek, walnut and Gubeen crêpe ¶ Potato and blue cheese cakes ¶ Asparagus, chard and goats' brie crêpe ¶ Goats' cheese, pinenut and oven-roasted tomato charlotte ¶ Roasted sweet pepper rolls of caper-pinenut stuffing ¶ Coconut-cumin pancakes ¶ Pastry and a couple of tarts ¶ Risotto ¶ Asparagus, mangetout and pinenut risotto ¶ Watercress and red onion risotto ¶ Radicchio and roasted pumpkin risotto ¶ Roasted roots and couscous pilaff ¶ Penne with fennel, green peppers, olives ¶ Pasta ribbons in lemon sauce ¶ Pasta in basil oil ¶ Moroccan-spiced vegetable and almond pastries ¶ Pumpkin, almond and spring cabbage dolma ¶ Couscous-crusted aubergine ¶ Thai tofu-cashew fritters ¶ Pistachio, green chilli and yoghurt kofta ¶ Aubergine gamelastra ¶ Gingered kale, walnut and pumpkin gratin ¶ Roast pumpkin with lemon-hazelnut risotto stuffing ¶

Roasted vegetable ratatouille and grilled ciabatta with olive and goats' cheese

I have no particular axe to grind about ratatouille, but I'm sure it was never meant to become that polite little mound of just-done dice beside your dinner in nice restaurants. I think of it as a stew of sun-ripened vegetables of the Mediterranean, rich and hearty, the vegetables just the other side of done, a sublime lunch for a lazy summer day. I've never eaten ratatouille in France, so I'm making this up, but I don't think of our version as French at all, so that's okay. The ciabatta with goats' cheese makes a meal of it, but any crusty bread, some salad leaves and a bottle of wine would do.

FOR FOUR TO SIX:

- 500g aubergines
- olive oil
- 1–2 sprigs of fresh rosemary or thyme
- 400g courgettes
- 200g green peppers
- 10 cloves garlic
- 1 onion
- 8 tomatoes
- 100mls red wine
- a handful of torn fresh herbs, such as parsley, basil, marjoram, oregano
- salt and pepper
- 1 large ciabatta loaf
- 4 tblspns olive tapenade (see page 35)
- 150g goats' cheese

CUT THE AUBERGINE INTO CHUNKS of about one inch, toss with plenty of olive oil in a roasting tray, add the rosemary and/or thyme and cook in a hot oven, turning the chunks often until well cooked, about 15–20 minutes.

Cut the courgette and pepper into slightly smaller chunks, as they will shrink less in the cooking. Cook them together in the same way, using just enough oil to coat the vegetables this time. Peel the garlic cloves, slice them in half (or not, if you wish) and add the slices to the courgettes and peppers after about five minutes' cooking. Remove this tray from the oven before the garlic starts to burn; unlike the aubergine, these vegetables can be considered cooked at almost any stage, to your liking or convenience.

Meanwhile, make a sauce to put the roasted vegetables in. Thickly slice the onion and cook it in a little olive oil in a large pan, until soft. Chop the tomatoes coarsely, add them to the pan with the wine, and cook over a moderate heat until the tomatoes have broken down a little and the sauce thickens slightly. Stir in the fresh herbs, season well, then add the vegetables. Reheat the ratatouille gently, and simmer for no more than five minutes. Scatter torn basil leaves over the top, just before serving.

Cut the ciabatta in half lengthways, spread a thin layer of tapenade on both halves, drizzle some olive oil over that and lay some thin slices of goats' cheese on top. Place under a hot grill until the cheese starts to brown. Cut into chunks and share it out.

Herbed potato tortilla

with avocado salsa

We've made a lot of different versions of these big, Spanish-style omelettes at Café Paradiso over the years. Sometimes, if we stray too far from the basic potato egg thing, we use the Italian word 'frittata' instead. The Spanish are very fussy about their classic, simple food being messed with; the Italians only pretend to be. This recipe is a straightforward version, with only the addition of some herbs. Once you can make this, you can experiment away to your heart's content. I learned to make a Spanish tortilla from a young woman in the Basque country. She was talking and moving fast, but I think I got the gist. The potatoes are important. Spanish recipes recommend using floury potatoes, and what they mean by floury our mothers wouldn't let inside the door! I've found that the perfect potato for tortilla is a Red Rooster, registering at halfway on the floury scale. This recipe will feed as many people as you need it to, ideally five or six.

FOR ONE 24cm TORTILLA:

- 500g potatoes, peeled
- 1 onion
- 4 cloves of garlic
- 7 eggs
- salt and pepper
- fresh herbs chopped – 2–3 sprigs of parsley, dill, oregano, marjoram, basil
- avocado salsa (see page 33)

AVOCADO SALSA:

(See page 33)

SLOWLY HEAT A HEAVY FRYING PAN and pour in about half an inch of olive oil. Thinly slice the onion and garlic. Cut the potatoes into pieces about the length of a matchstick and twice as thick – a very thin chip. Add the potatoes, onion and garlic to the pan and turn up the heat so that the potatoes are practically deep-frying. They will need a bit of attention at this stage to prevent them sticking to the pan or to each other.

Meanwhile, whisk the eggs in a large bowl. Keep returning to the eggs for an occasional whisk, while the potatoes cook. When the potatoes are soft on the inside and beginning to colour, strain off most of the oil and tip them with the herbs and lots of salt and pepper into the egg, stirring briskly – the heat of the potatoes will begin to cook the egg, but that's to your advantage if it happens evenly rather than scrambling in spots, so pay attention and move quickly at this stage.

Wipe the pan with a towel, brush it with a thin coat of clean olive oil and return it to the stove, over a low heat this time. Pour in the egg mixture and use a slice or spatula to tuck down the edge and flatten the top. Leave it for five minutes or so before lifting the edge to have a peek at the bottom. Ideally, with a low, even heat and a fine thick, well-seasoned pan, the tortilla will be quite set most of the way to the top when the bottom begins to brown. Loosen the tortilla with the slice or spatula, slide it out on to a large plate, invert the pan over the tortilla and quickly flip the whole lot over so that the top of the tortilla is now nestling in the pan. A few minutes over low heat should finish the cooking – in fact, I often turn the heat off and leave the pan over the cooling stove for about five minutes. If the bottom is browning but the tortilla is still wet, a useful idea is to put the pan under a grill for a few minutes to set the top, before going ahead with the flip. Slide the tortilla back on to the plate before slicing it – you don't want to damage your precious pan.

Squash, butterbean and leek stew

with rosemary and chilli and Gabriel cheese gougeres

This wasn't the first stew I'd done with these cute little choux pastries, but they're so well met that I may have to leave them alone together. The stew is very simply flavoured with totally harmonious ingredients, true comfort food if you keep the chilli levels down to heartwarming. For colour and texture, try to use a few types of squash, from those with pale green, firm flesh, like Acorns or Butternut, to the deep oranges of Hokaido or the grey-skinned Crowns, but always use an orange-fleshed one for the stock. The recipe was inspired by Ian Flanagan who brought me a magazine piece on squashes after he had made a soup-stew crossbreed from it. My recipe uses a different method, partly because of the logistics of catering, but more because I've been gradually changing my approach to stews in general. I still love a stew (or curry) which has been simmered for ages and left out in the rain for two days, but now I make most stews by preparing a background sauce and part-cooking the vegetables separately, then bringing them together for a shorter time. When it works, you have greater control over how cooked the vegetables become, some distinct flavours and still the essence of a stew – a mingling of flavours in the background stock. The gougeres are basic choux pastries with as much cheese as the dough will take. Gabriel is a hard, mature cheese from West Cork, with a slightly sharp, peppery flavour. If you fancy the stew but the gougeres make you nervous, eat it with warm bread, garlic or cheese-toasted bread, or rice.

FOR FOUR:

- 60g butterbeans
- boiling water
- 400g orange-fleshed squash or pumpkin
- 1 litre light stock
- 1 onion, halved
- 2 whole dried chillies
- 2 bay leaves
- 1 tsp salt
- 3 sprigs fresh rosemary
- 600g squash
- 400g leeks
- 10 cloves garlic
- 4 tblspns olive oil
- 2 fresh mild chillies
- 50mls white wine

SOAK THE BUTTERBEANS in cold water for four hours or overnight, rinse them and cook in plenty of boiling water until tender; one to two hours.

To get about 400g of pumpkin flesh for the stock, you will need to peel and deseed a pumpkin of about 600–700g. Unless the skin is very thin, peeling means slicing the skin off, carefully, with a knife. Carefully chop the pumpkin in half first, scoop out all the seeds and stringy stuff, then take the skin off with a knife. It may help to chop the pumpkin into even smaller pieces first. Then chop the peeled pumpkin coarsely and put it in a pot with the stock, onion, whole chillies, bay leaves, one teaspoon of salt and two sprigs of the rosemary. Bring it to the boil and simmer on a low heat for half an hour. Remove the chilli, bay leaves and rosemary stalks (it doesn't matter if you lose some of the rosemary itself in the stock), then puree the rest. This is the base of the stew and can be made up to a day before. Meanwhile, prepare the 600g of squash or squashes in the same way, cutting the flesh into two-bite pieces.

Wash and trim the leeks, but leave them as intact as possible, then slice them into large rounds, 2–3cm long, depending on their diameter. Use as much of the green part as possible too, it is a little tougher but at least as flavoursome as the white part. Peel the garlic cloves and slice them thickly or halve them. Now, gently stew the leeks and garlic in the olive oil until the leeks soften a little but are still short of tender; no more than five minutes. The smell will make you ravenous but persist. Slice the fresh chillies, discarding the seeds if you wish, and add them to the pot with the wine and the squash pieces. Stew for another five minutes or so, while you bring the pumpkin stock back to the boil.

Take the rosemary needles off the last stalk and add them to the leeks with the pumpkin stock and the butterbeans. Simmer it, uncovered, until the squashes are just tender. At a low simmer, this should take about 20–30 minutes. If you sense that the squashes are cooking before the stock reduces and thickens to your satisfaction, finish the cooking at a faster boil. The squashes can happily break down a little at the edges, harmonising with the stock and helping it to thicken. Check the seasoning before serving – it's not too late to add a little spice or salt.

FOR THE GOUGERES:

- 110g strong white flour
- 170mls water
- 60g butter
- 2 medium eggs
- 80g Gabriel cheese
- small bunch fresh chives, finely chopped
- ½ tsp salt
- pinch of cayenne pepper

PREHEAT THE OVEN to 380°F. Line a baking tray with baking parchment. Sift the flour and put it in a food processor. Bring the water and butter to a rolling boil and tip it quickly into the processor with the motor running. Leave it running, wait thirty seconds, then crack in one egg. Wait for this to be incorporated before adding the next egg. Allow this to become well incorporated before adding the Gabriel cheese and some seasoning. Quickly pipe or spoon sixteen small mounds or crescent shapes onto a baking tray, leaving a little room for expansion, and place the tray in the oven. Check after eight minutes, you may need to turn individual gougeres for even cooking, and turn the oven down to 350°F. Bake for another five minutes, check again, and if they seem well risen, firm and capable of supporting themselves, make a small slit in the side of each and return them to the oven for a further three minutes, which you can now turn down to 300°F. This should dry the gougeres a little to prevent them collapsing later. The gougeres are best made fresh, though they reheat well from the freezer, if they are frozen shortly after being made.

Serve generous portions of the slightly wet stew and tuck three or four of the gougeres into each portion.

Mushroom, pak choy and eggroll stir fry

with buckwheat noodles and a sweet ginger and chilli sauce

This dish is about the buckwheat noodles even more than any of the other interesting ingredients. I love buckwheat, especially for winter pilaffs with mushrooms, dill, fennel, yoghurt and the like, but it's very hard to find an audience for that kind of thing in a restaurant, while everyone loves noodles. Don't buy the 100 per cent buckwheat variety - they are impossible to cook - Japanese 40 per cent are best. If you can't read the instructions, cook them like spaghetti in lots of boiling water, checking them often, and cool them under cold water to stop the cooking. The quantities here are approximate minimum amounts per person. To be honest, it's hard to conceive of doing this for more than two in a wok. I cook stir fries one at a time (or in up to three separate woks, if necessary) so if you're frying for more than two, prepare everything first and do one or two portions at a time. In any case, it is good practice for all stir frying to prepare everything before frying, thus allowing you to concentrate on the wok. The sauce recipe makes about 1 litre, enough for eight to ten people, and it keeps and reheats very well. Make sure it's hot when it hits the wok or it will slow the dish to a simmering stew instead of a stir fry.

FOR THE SAUCE:

- 2 onions
- 1 fennel bulb or 2 sticks of celery
- 10 garlic cloves, peeled
- 4 whole chillies
- 1.2 litres light stock
- 2 tblspns grated ginger
- 1 tblspns sambal oelek
- 100mls tomato passata
- 1 tblspns shoyu
- 2 tsps cornflour

PER PERSON:

- 1 egg
- 50g buckwheat noodles
- ½ onion
- 150g mushrooms
- 150g pak choy

CHOP THE ONION AND FENNEL INTO QUARTERS, put them in a pot with the garlic, chillies and the stock, bring it to the boil and simmer for half an hour over a very low heat. Then strain off the solids and return the liquid to the pot. Add the ginger, the sambal, tomato and shoyu, and simmer for another ten minutes or so. Mix the cornflour with a little cold water, stir it into the stock and simmer for five minutes more. Reheat as much as you need, in a small pan, as you cook the stir fry.

To make the eggrolls, lightly beat the egg(s), with some salt and pepper. In a non-stick or crêpe pan, make thin pancakes – you should get two per egg. You can either flip the pancake over for a few seconds, or use a slice to roll it up in the pan as it cooks – this gives a softer, fatter roll. Slice the eggrolls into strips. This can be done up to a few hours before you finish the stir fry.

Cook the buckwheat noodles, rinse them in cold water, and drain them. Slice the onion very thinly in quarter rounds. How you slice the mushrooms depends on the variety you use – moist, fast-cooking ones, like oysters can be left whole or halved, others may need to be sliced thinly. Slice the stalk of the pak choy diagonally about 1cm thick and tear the leaves coarsely. Heat some cooking oil to a high temperature in a wok, toss in the onion and fry it for a minute, stirring with a tongs or chopsticks. Now toss in the mushrooms and pak choy and fry on, keeping the temperature high and the vegetables moving. Just as the vegetables are done, throw in the eggrolls, the cooked noodles and about 100mls of hot sauce per person. Heat this through, mixing the noodles and vegetables together as you go, then tip it out on to plates. Now, if you're cooking for more than two, go and do it all again. Who'd be a cook, as my mother would say.

Noodles, tofu, leeks and greens

in coconut sauce with lime and coriander

A soothing noodle dish, where the vegetables are simmered gently in a thin coconut sauce and finished with the enlivening flavours of lime juice and fresh coriander. It is served fairly wet, halfway to soup, so give people spoons to go with their forks or chopsticks. If you don't have a fresh chilli to hand, use a dried one, either finely ground or left whole, and take it out when the vegetables go in. This is a mild dish, but feel free to increase the chilli levels if you want something more exciting. The vegetables too can be varied; green beans, radishes, fennel and thinly sliced roots are all good, though I think it works best with only two or three types. If you don't use leeks add a little onion to the vegetables or some scallions at the end.

FOR FOUR:

- 100g tofu
- 50mls pineapple juice
- juice of 1 lime
- 700mls water or light stock
- 1 tblspn grated ginger
- 1 large fresh chilli, seeded and thinly sliced
- 4 cloves of garlic, finely chopped
- 2 tsps coriander seeds, ground
- 80g creamed coconut
- 1 tsp tomato puree
- 1 tblspn soya sauce
- 1 small carrot
- 1 leek, about 150g
- 100g cabbage – savoy, spring green, kale or any oriental cabbage
- 1 pack of thin egg noodles
- 2 limes
- small handful of fresh coriander

THE TOFU SHOULD BE CUT INTO SMALL DICE and marinated for at least two hours. Use the marinade on page 128 or simply dilute some shoyu with water and add a little grated ginger. Take the dice from the marinade, drain them for a minute on paper or cloth, then fry them in hot oil until lightly browned.

To start the sauce, place the juices in a pan with 200mls of the water, the ginger, chilli, garlic and coriander. Bring to the boil and simmer over a low heat for eight to ten minutes. Chop the creamed coconut and add it to the pan with the tomato puree, soya sauce and the rest of the water. Bring back to the boil and simmer again for a further five minutes.

Meanwhile, slice the carrot in half lengthways, cut these pieces in half across, then slice these into thin strips. Slice the leek and the cabbage into similar strips. Put the vegetables into the coconut sauce and bring it back to the boil. Tough cabbage, and savoy often is, is best cooked separately first in boiling water for a minute to soften and shrink it a little. Spring greens or any oriental greens can go straight into the coconut sauce with the rest of the vegetables. Simmer very gently for a few minutes, until the cabbage, leeks and pepper are tender. If you do this very gently, the vegetables will cook slowly, absorbing the flavours of the stock, without boiling away the liquid. Add the fried tofu for the last minute of cooking.

Meanwhile, cook the noodles according to the pack instructions, then stir them into the cooked vegetables, using tongs or chopsticks to mix everything thoroughly. Use tongs to share the noodles and vegetables between four plates, then pour over the sauce left behind in the pan. This can be a messy procedure when you've got more than two portions in the pot, and a less stressful approach is to divide the cooked noodles between four bowls, pour the vegetables and sauce over them and do the mixing in the bowls, or even leave everybody to their own mixing. Offer halved limes, to be squeezed over the dish, and lots of chopped fresh coriander.

Baked leek, walnut and Gubeen crêpe

with a puy lentil, tomato and kale concasse

Food for a winter's evening: leeks, walnuts, mustard and lightly smoked Gubeen cheese. We sometimes serve this crêpe with mushrooms in a dilled cream sauce and with some flageolet beans. The effect is similar to this version in that the accompanying vegetables double as a sauce for the crêpe.

THE FILLING:

- 600g leeks
- 6 cloves of garlic, chopped
- tblspn butter
- 50mls white wine
- 2 tsps Dijon or strong Irish mustard
- 50mls single cream
- 80g smoked Gubeen cheese, diced
- 40g walnuts, lightly roasted and coarsely chopped
- salt and pepper

FOR THE CRÊPES:

- 100g plain flour
- 1 egg
- 250mls milk
- salt and pepper

FOR THE CONCASSE:

- 4–8 leaves of Italian black kale or Irish curly kale
- 2 cloves garlic, chopped
- 1 red onion, finely chopped
- 200mls olive oil
- 2 tomatoes, seeded and diced
- 4 tblspns cooked puy lentils
- salt and pepper

WASH THE LEEKS, then slice them thinly. Stew the leeks and garlic in a tablespoon of butter for five minutes. Add the wine and mustard, increase the heat and cook for a further five minutes or so, stirring, until the leeks are just tender. Pour in the cream and cook on high for one more minute. Allow this to cool before stirring in the cheese, walnuts and some seasoning.

YOU WILL NEED ONE LARGE CRÊPE for each person. This recipe will make more, but leaves room for error and the leftover crêpes will keep for a few days. Sift the flour, whisk the egg and milk together briefly with a little seasoning, then whisk this liquid into the flour, without overbeating. You will get a slightly better crêpe if you leave the batter to stand for half an hour now, but if you're impatient, carry on, no one will notice. Fry the crêpes in your special iron pan which you keep just for crêpes (of course you do), allowing them to colour only lightly, as they will have to withstand a period in the oven later.

Preheat an oven to 350°F (Gas Mark 4). To assemble the crêpe: thinking of it as four quarters, place some filling in the top two quarters, extending to the edges but leaving a gap in the middle. Fold up the bottom half of the crêpe, pressing gently to give a fairly even distribution of the filling. Then fold the crêpe again along the gap left between the top quarters, to get a well-filled triangular parcel. Repeat with the other crêpes. Brush the tops with a little olive oil or butter and bake in the warm oven until warmed through and beginning to crisp, about 15 minutes.

COOK THE KALE IN BOILING WATER for two or three minutes, then chop it coarsely. Stew the garlic and onion in a tablespoon of the olive oil for a minute, then stir in kale, tomatoes, lentils, seasoning and the rest of the olive oil. Cook this for a further minute, just to heat everything through.

Slide the crêpes on to four warmed plates and ladle the concasse over and around them. A few tiny roast potatoes tucked into the concasse will finish this warming winter dish nicely, or else serve a mountain of boiled, roast or mashed spuds communally.

Potato and blue cheese cakes

with flageolet beans in cider and rosemary

Inside the crisp coating of these fried cakes the comforting potato mash is broken up by tangy pockets of melting blue cheese. It is important to use a fairly strong cheese with plenty of blue veining, otherwise the cakes will be all comfort and no character. Stilton is perfect, both because it is usually sold when fairly mature and strong and because its dry, crumbly nature doesn't soften the mash. If you use an Irish blue, buy it from a cheese counter where you can test it first, as the stuff in the supermarket is often too young and mild. The fresh herbs are optional, though one or all of them will add a sparkle of freshness to these very wintry cakes. The flageolet bean dish is a richly flavoured way to present beans as a side dish. This quantity will easily satisfy four people, maybe more. It can also form the basis of a more substantial stew, with the addition of other vegetables, such as leek, fennel, mushrooms, green beans and peppers, even squashes. Here, the dish is finished to a fairly dry, intense consistency, but if you want to make it wetter simply stop the liquid reduction earlier and/or add more cream at the finish.

FOR FOUR (TWELVE CAKES):

- 650g floury potatoes
- 1 tblspn butter, about 25g
- 2 spring onions, finely chopped
- 4 cloves garlic, finely chopped
- ¼ tsp nutmeg
- salt and pepper
- small handful of fresh dill, chives and parsley, chopped
- 120g blue cheese, crumbled
- 1 egg yolk
- 150g breadcrumbs
- 50g plain flour
- 1 egg, beaten with 100mls milk

BOIL AND MASH THE POTATOES with the butter. There are detailed instructions for potato mashing in the wasabi mash recipe on page 23. Cook the spring onion and garlic for a minute in a little butter, then stir it into the potato with the nutmeg, seasoning and some fresh herbs if you have them. Leave this mash to cool before gently stirring in the cheese and the egg yolk. The cheese should remain in uneven crumbled lumps scattered through the mash. It's best if this is done a good few hours ahead, even the day before if that suits you, but no more than that.

Divide the mash into twelve pieces, then use your hands to make these into nice even-shaped cakes. Coat these in breadcrumbs by first tossing them in the flour, then dipping them in the egg and milk and finally in the crumbs. Make sure that the mash is well coated all over.

Heat some cooking oil in a wide frying pan, enough to come halfway up the cakes. Fry a batch of cakes, well spaced, at a fairly high temperature for about five minutes on each side. If you overcrowd the pan or cook the cakes too gently, they will fall apart or absorb more oil than you'll want to eat. The balance you want to get is the cakes frying to a crisp, golden finish all round while heating all the way through. They will keep warm for a short while in a low to moderate oven, a few minutes after that they will fall apart.

Serve three cakes per person with some of the flageolet beans and maybe some buttered leeks to prop them up.

FLAGEOLET BEANS FOR FOUR TO SIX:

- 250g flageolet beans, soaked overnight in cold water
- 300mls dry cider

RINSE THE BEANS and put them in a large pot with plenty of cold water, bring it to the boil and skim off any froth that develops, then simmer until the beans are tender. This can take anything from 40 minutes to two hours, depending on the age of the beans. Drain the beans and put them in a smaller pan with the cider, stock, garlic and

- 200mls stock or water
- 4 cloves garlic, sliced
- 1 sprig of fresh rosemary
- 2 tomatoes, deseeded
- 100mls single cream
- salt and pepper

rosemary. Bring this to the boil and cook at a lively simmer (but no faster – it should take at least ten minutes to allow the beans to absorb the flavours) until the liquid has reduced to a level just covering the beans. Now chop the tomato flesh, add it to the pot and simmer for two minutes.

Everything up to this point can be done in advance and left to sit until you are ready to serve. To finish the stew, pour the cream into the beans with a little salt and pepper, bring it back to the boil and cook briskly for a minute. The resulting stew should be rich and not too wet.

Asparagus, chard and goats' brie crêpe

with rocket pesto

There's a crêpe for every season, and this one is late spring. The Irish goats' milk brie that we use for this has some of the creaminess of ordinary brie and just a hint of that special goat thing that people either love or hate. If you can keep the portion size down, this makes an exquisite starter. However, we usually cram the crêpes and serve one each with the peppery rocket pesto and some buttered new potatoes. This recipe makes enough for four.

SEE PAGE 101 FOR THE CRÊPES

FOR THE FILLING:

- 400g chard
- 1 onion, finely chopped
- 4 cloves garlic, finely chopped
- 1 tsp butter
- 2 tomatoes, seeded and diced
- 1 tsp strong Irish mustard, or Dijon
- 100mls single cream
- salt and pepper
- 200g asparagus
- 150g goats' brie
- rocket pesto, (see page 37)

COOK THE CHARD by dropping it into boiling water for 30 seconds, then cool it immediately in cold water. Chop it coarsely. Cook the onion and garlic in a little butter until soft, add the tomatoes and mustard, cook for one minute more, then pour in the cream and boil it for half a minute. Season the sauce and stir it into the chard.

Cook the asparagus by boiling it gently until just tender, then chop it into inch-long pieces, leaving the heads intact.

To assemble the crêpes, approach each one as four quarters, place some chard in the top two quarters, extending to the edges but leaving a gap in the middle. Cover these layers with a generous amount of asparagus, then top that with thin slices of the cheese. Fold up the bottom half of the crêpe, pressing gently to give a fairly even distribution of the filling. Then fold the crêpe again along the gap left between the top quarters, to get a well-filled triangular parcel. Repeat with the other crêpes. Brush the crêpes with a little butter and bake them until warmed through and beginning to crisp, about 15 minutes.

Serve the crêpes with one or two tablespoons of rocket pesto as a sauce for each, some new potatoes and salad.

Roasted sweet pepper rolls of caper-pinenut stuffing

with a roasted garlic-chive cream, lemon risotto and sugar snaps

I've given this dish its full descriptive name here, as it appears occasionally during the summer on the Paradiso menu, because it is the combination and contrast of flavours that creates an overall effect above and beyond the sum of the parts. That's not to say that the pepper rolls aren't good with other dishes, or that the lemon risotto isn't very useful on lots of menus; if you like roasted garlic, the sauce can become addictive and you'll find yourself dunking bread into it. But, from what I've witnessed, what excites people about the dish is the variety of tastes and textures which contrast and complement each other. There are very strong sweet flavours, the acid of the lemon and the capers, the rich intensity of the cream, and the soothing calm of the risotto with a pile of sweet, crunchy sugar snaps on top of it, insisting that it is mid-summer, after all. This is a very important role for short-season vegetables, especially on a rain-washed July evening in Cork, when sometimes the only difference between summer and winter is the food on the table. Sugar snaps say it loudest, but mangetout, green beans, even spinach, chard and the like are fine substitutes if they are fresh and barely cooked.

FOR FOUR:

- 1 onion, finely chopped
- 2 garlic cloves, finely chopped
- 1 tblspn butter
- 80mls single cream
- 1 tsp hot mustard, Dijon or similar
- 40g pinenuts, lightly toasted
- 40g capers
- 100g breadcrumbs
- parsley, chopped
- black pepper, to taste
- 6 red or yellow peppers
- risotto from 150g arborio rice

- 150g sugar snaps or mangetout

COOK THE ONION AND GARLIC in a tablespoon of butter until the onion has softened. Pour in the cream and the mustard, bring it to the boil and simmer until it has reduced to a thick sauce, about five minutes. Leave the sauce to cool before stirring in the pinenuts, capers, breadcrumbs and some chopped parsley. Season with black pepper, but be careful with salt – the capers may already have brought enough to the dish.

Meanwhile, roast and peel the peppers, then cut each in half. Many peppers seem to fall naturally into three pieces, so it might be safer to slice the peppers in two before peeling.

Place a couple of teaspoons of the filling, pressed together, along one side edge of each pepper piece (if you take the stem end as the top and the edges perpendicular to it as sides, that is), and carefully roll the pepper, manipulating the filling as you go, to make sure that the shape you end up with is well filled. Usually, there will be just enough pepper to wrap itself around the filling. Place the filled peppers, seam side down, on a baking tray lined with parchment or greaseproof paper. Brush them lightly with olive oil and bake them in a moderately hot oven for ten minutes. They will hold well for longer in a low oven, if you need them to while you make the risotto and cook the sugar snaps.

Serve three rolls per person, with some garlic cream spooned over them, the risotto and a pile of barely cooked sugar snaps.

WITHOUT REMOVING THEIR SKINS, toss the garlic cloves in a little olive oil and roast them in a moderate oven until the cloves have become soft and lightly browned, but not crisped. When they are cool enough to handle, squeeze the garlic cloves from their skins and put them in a pot with the wine and stock. Simmer this for a

ROASTED GARLIC-CHIVE CREAM:

- 10 garlic cloves
- a little olive oil
- 80mls white wine
- 150mls light stock
- 150mls single cream
- fresh chives, chopped
- 1 lemon rind and juice
- salt and pepper
- sugar snaps, to serve
- risotto, to serve

few minutes, then blend together. (You could also sieve out any surviving pieces of garlic, but I wouldn't bother.) Add the cream and fresh chives, bring the sauce back to the boil and simmer until the cream has thickened to your satisfaction. I like this to be quite thick, for the intensity of flavour and so that a small amount can be kept in the vicinity of the peppers on the plate. Season with caution.

The lemon risotto is simply a basic risotto with lemon rind and juice added in with the final ladle of stock. Follow risotto instructions on page 112. As a side dish for four people, you will need a risotto made from about 150g rice, and the juice and rind of one lemon. If you have any fresh fennel herb available, I think it goes really well with the lemon in the risotto.

Coconut-cumin pancakes

with aubergine and cabbage, coriander-lime oil and chilli-roasted squash

The recipe for these pancakes is adapted from one for 'serabi', Indonesian breakfast pancakes, which I learned while catering for a gamelan performance. That day we served them topped delicately with a tropical fruit puree and fresh mango, but changed the recipe next day to a savoury version and have subjected them ever since to all sorts of heavily spiced partners, mostly this very rich aubergine concoction. The aubergine stew itself has had many lives already, with a few changes, as a pasta sauce and pastry filling amongst others. I like the aubergine to be very hot with chillies, some of which is absorbed by the pancakes underneath and is also offset by serving it with the relative calm of gingered squash and a few blobs of soured cream around the plate for dipping into. I would make the pancakes and the stew anything up to a day ahead and reheat them while the squash is roasting. The recipe for this is on page 27.

FOR 24 PANCAKES, ABOUT EIGHT TO TEN PORTIONS:

- 100g strong flour
- 100g rice flour
- ¼ tsp salt
- 2 dstspns ground cumin seeds
- 1 egg
- 400mls coconut milk
- chopped fresh coriander

FOR THE FILLING:

- 250g aubergine
- 1 tblspn olive oil
- 1 onion, finely chopped
- 5 cloves garlic, crushed
- 2 sprigs of fresh thyme
- 1 tsp cumin seeds
- ½ tsp chopped hot chillies
- 1 tsp coriander seeds, ground
- 2 ripe tomatoes
- 50mls red wine
- 1 tsp tomato puree
- ¼ tsp salt
- savoy cabbage, kale or spring cabbage, about 100g
- coriander-lime oil, (see page 40)
- chilli-roasted squash (see page 27)

SIFT THE FLOURS, SALT AND CUMIN. Whisk the egg into the coconut milk, then whisk this into the flours. Stir in the coriander. This should give you a thick pouring batter, which makes a pancake a good deal thicker than the average crêpe. Heat a large frying pan to a medium-low heat. Brush it very lightly with oil, then pour in one to three small ladlefuls of the batter, about one tablespoon each to give a diameter of about 6cm. Fry the pancakes for about two minutes, then flip them over and fry the other side. Turn them out on to a plate in a random pile – they won't stick to each other. This will make more than you need for now, but they keep well and it's hard to make a smaller batter.

CHOP THE AUBERGINE into very small dice, toss in olive oil and roast in a moderate oven, until cooked through. It will need a bit of attention and turning to avoid scorching, due to the size of the dice.

Meanwhile, start the sauce by cooking the onion in a little olive oil for a minute, then add the garlic, herbs and spices. Chop the tomatoes into small dice and add them, with the wine and puree, to the pot when the onion is soft. Cook over a moderate heat until reduced to a thick sauce, about half an hour. Check for all the flavours – it should be very hot with chilli, but that's up to you at this stage. Add in the roasted aubergine, and bring to the boil for a minute. Chop the cabbage into short, thin shreds and drop it into boiling water for a minute or so, then stir it into the aubergine. Keep this warm over a low heat, while you reheat the pancakes. When the pancakes are warm, pile a generous amount of filling on each, about a tablespoon, then put three overlapping pancakes on each plate. Spoon some of the coriander-lime oil around and over each portion, add a few blobs of soured cream or yoghurt, if you like; then arrange the chilli-roasted squash around the plate.

Pastry and a couple of tarts

I well remember the first time I made good pastry, that is pastry that added pleasures of taste and texture to the tart as distinct from just holding up the filling. I threw the wholemeal flour in the bin, got out a book and read about pastry. This told me what I was supposed to be trying to do, what I didn't want to happen, and gave a basic set of quantities. It worked, and afterwards I felt like I'd made a quantum leap out of a cooking corner. With a little information, pastry is about confidence, definitely something you can't do in fear. While pastry doesn't have the sensual pleasures of breadmaking, there is the smug satisfaction to be had, at each stage, of sensing that everything is going perfectly. In a way, pastry makes itself in the sense that it would be perfect if you could bring the ingredients together in the shape you want at the first stroke. The difficulty for a cook is to avoid damaging it along the way. Kneading, rolling and, handling of any kind is not adding to the quality of the pastry, only changing its shape, and should be done as quickly, efficiently and calmly as possible. The main dangers to your pastry are putting too much water in, which makes it easy to roll but evaporates in the cooking, causing shrinking; using butter which is not cold enough or warming it in the process by overhandling or taking too long in a warm environment, which will mess with the texture and give you dense or cardboard-like pastry; any kind of overstretching while rolling or pressing the pastry into the case – it will look all right but revert and shrink to its natural shape in the cooking. Once you've made pastry that is crisp, flaky and melts in the mouth a few times, it becomes second nature and would require a crisis of confidence to take it away.

FOR ONE 9"/23cm PASTRY CASE:

- 120g plain flour
- large pinch salt
- 60g cold butter
- 30mls/2 tblspns cold water

SIFT THE FLOUR AND SALT, then cut in the butter until you get a breadcrumb-like texture. This much can be done very efficiently in a food processor. The rest is best done by hand so tip the 'crumbs' into a bowl, make a well in the centre and pour in the water. Quickly mix it in with a few strokes of a wooden spoon. When it has roughly come together, use your hands to knead the dough very briefly to get a smooth ball. Wrap and chill this for at least half an hour. If you chill it for much longer, allow it to sit at room temperature for a little while before rolling it.

On a lightly floured surface, roll the dough to fit the tart case comfortably. I turn the pastry through 90 degrees after each roll and I think this helps to get an even thickness and to avoid the pastry sticking and thus stretching or tearing. Lay the rolled pastry into the case and gently nudge it into the edges, without stretching the dough. Trim off the excess dough and prick the base a few times with a fork to liberate any air bubbles you may have missed. Wrap the pastry again and chill for a further half hour. At this stage, it also freezes well and can be used straight from the freezer. To 'blind' bake the pastry, line the base with baking parchment, cover this with some dried beans, and bake at about 350°F (Gas Mark 4) for seven to ten minutes. The pastry is now ready to accommodate whatever filling you wish to treat it to.

Spinach, leek and stilton tart

A winter tart with the familiar, comforting flavours of leeks and blue cheese. I use stilton for cooking because of its dry texture and richly 'blue' flavour. We usually serve this with some sundried tomato pesto (see page 38) and braised puy lentils (see page 25), or some roasted root vegetables.

FOR FIVE TO SIX:

- one 23cm pastry case
- 300g spinach
- 250g leeks, in thin rounds
- 4 garlic cloves, chopped
- 250g stilton, crumbled
- ¼ tsp nutmeg
- ¼ tsp black pepper
- 2 eggs
- 200mls single cream

PREHEAT AN OVEN to 350°F (Gas Mark 4). Prepare a pastry case and blind bake it, as described opposite.

Cook the spinach in boiling water for about 30 seconds, then cool it in cold water. Squeeze all the water out of the spinach, then chop it coarsely and set it aside in a bowl. Meanwhile cook the leeks and garlic in a little butter until the leeks are tender but not soft, then add this to the spinach with the leeks, cheese and seasonings. Whisk together the eggs and cream, then stir most of this custard into the vegetables. Pile this filling into a pre-baked pastry case, pour the rest of the custard over the top and bake the tart for about 30 minutes, until it is just set and lightly browned on top. Leave the tart to stand for five minutes before slicing it.

Aubergine, tomato & mozzarella tart

A summer tart, though still a very substantial one with roasted aubergines, cheese, eggs and cream. Serve this with a simple salad or lightly cooked greens and either a pesto or the fennel-chilli salsa (see page 33).

FOR FIVE TO SIX:

- 1 23cm pastry case
- 2 medium aubergines
- 6–8 tomatoes
- a little salt and pepper
- 1 small bunch of fresh basil
- 300g mozzarella, sliced
- a little parmesan
- 2 eggs
- 300mls single cream

PREHEAT AN OVEN to 350°F (Gas Mark 4). Prepare a pastry case and blind-bake it (see page 110). Slice the aubergines into rounds, about 10mm thick, brush both sides of the slices with olive oil and roast them on an oven tray, until lightly browned and cooked through. Slice the tomatoes the same thickness and remove the seeds. Roast them in the same way. Place a layer of slightly overlapping aubergine slices in the bottom of the pastry case. Arrange a layer of tomatoes on top, sprinkle with salt, pepper and some torn basil leaves, then put in a layer of mozzarella slices. Sprinkle a little grated parmesan over this. Whisk the eggs and cream together and pour half of this custard over the vegetables. Put in another layer of aubergine, some more basil, a layer of tomatoes on top, and a final sprinkling of seasoning and parmesan. Now pour in as much of the remaining custard as the tart will take - it should take it all. Carefully place the tart in the oven and bake it for 30–40 minutes, until the custard has just set. The tart will firm up perfectly if you leave it to rest for five to ten minutes before you slice it, and it will also taste better for being a good few degrees down from oven-hot.

Risotto

Two risotto memories invariably come to me when I take out a bag of arborio rice. The first is of a fellow Irish tourist in a hotel dining room on the last night of a package holiday in Sicily, a middle-aged well-off sort, travelled and fond of his food: '. . . and what's more, the risotto was terrible, for God's sake, it was wet as soup'. Maybe the risotto was poor, but the waiter's eyes argued back that signor didn't know what he was talking about, and I remember wishing I had eaten the risotto so I would know both sides of the misunderstanding. The other is a book I seem to have mislaid, by Burton Anderson, about the author's visits to food artisans in Italy. He talked first to rice growers who spoke of good and bad paddy fields, vintage years and the merits and limitations of the many different risotto rices, not to mention the thousands of different varieties worldwide (most of which they, naturally, dismiss as not worth the trouble). Then he spoke to some of the best people cooking these rices in Italy. It's a mindboggling chapter that could easily make you give up altogether until you had your own paddy field, but somehow I came out of it with a strong sense of how I liked and wanted to cook risotto – a bit like your man there, but that other fellow has a point too. They didn't agree on much but you could tell they all made great risotto!

By the way, in passing it was pointed out by the rice growers that because of the amount of chemicals used in the production

of rice it is not a good idea to eat wholegrain rice unless it is certified organic. The husk diligently holds almost all the residual poisons. This, I'm sure you know, is also true of potatoes and root vegetables – don't eat the skin unless the label says organic.

One of the major arguing points about risotto concerns whether the rice should be cooked at a lively ping! ping! ping! rate with constant stirring or a slow plop plop plop with occasional gentle stirring. I tend to work somewhere in between, but closer to the lively end of the scale, but I know that the really critical things tend to be ones like whether you allow the rice to stick to the pan or stop simmering altogether. The most important thing, as in most cooking, is to have a clear understanding of what you are trying to achieve, then concentrate on getting there, and not end up somewhere else with a dish you don't like. And remember that nothing is written in stone, and that risotto is no more than an evolved way of cooking rice which probably did start out as soup.

Essentially, it has three stages: the initial toasting of the grains to seal in the starch and control its release; the braising with stock and wine; and at the end the addition of cheese, butter, olive oil, vegetables, herbs or whatever you fancy. It isn't really much harder than boiling potatoes, a small bit of care is all that's needed, but turn your back for too long and it's all gone horribly wrong. A lot is made of the importance of stock to a risotto, usually by cooks who've never had one without the overbearing taste of boiled dead animals. I hate it when rice tastes of boiled chicken or fish or even meat bones. Why should it? Especially if the main ingredient of the risotto is something so vivid and full of sunshine as peas, asparagus or mangetout. Some cooks, especially in restaurants, seem to become addicted to the flavour of chicken stock from their training and can't bring themselves to send food to the table without it. So often what a chef considers a subtle background flavour comes across to a clean palate as a bowl of rice, or soup, doing dead chicken impersonations. For some risotto I simply use a good vegetable stock cube with, perhaps, the cooking water of any pre-cooked vegetables being added, reduced a little if necessary. An exception is risotto with mushrooms which really does need a mushroom stock, and then the soaking water of a few dried mushrooms is fine.

One thing I wouldn't argue about with classic risotto recipes is the amount of cheese, butter and seasoning added at the end of the cooking, except that I tend to replace half the butter with olive oil. Not for any deluded notions about fats, but because Bridget has converted me to how well they work together in some circumstances. Fats in collusion. Strange notion. But, again, it's up to you how much butter, oil or cheese you add.

The first risotto recipe is as simple as risotto gets. After that you can make any risotto you like.

Asparagus, mangetout and pinenut risotto

with basil oil and roasted beetroot

This is a very simple, summer risotto which might also include peas, broad beans or sugar snaps with, or instead of, the mangetout or asparagus. We usually serve risotto with a little oil or pesto and one or two other vegetables on the side, to add a variety of taste and texture; in this case the beetroot. A simple salad of lettuce leaves is a perfect partner too.

FOR FOUR:

- 8–10 asparagus spears
- 1200mls stock
- 60mls olive oil
- 60g butter
- 1 onion, finely chopped
- 4 cloves of garlic, chopped
- 320g arborio or other risotto rice
- 120mls dry white wine
- 100g mangetout
- 2 tblspns pinenuts, lightly toasted
- 60g fresh parmesan, grated
- fresh basil, oregano, and/or parsley
- salt and pepper
- roasted beetroot (see page 21)
- basil oil (see page 39)

IF YOU ARE PLANNING TO SERVE THE ROASTED BEETROOT with this, start it first and if it is done too early, simply hold it in a warm oven until you want it.

Snap the tough ends off the asparagus spears and rinse them – asparagus can hold very fine grit, especially in the heads. Bring about 1200mls of water to the boil and cook the asparagus spears in it until just tender, then take them out, cool them in cold water and set them aside. Add some stock powder to the hot water and keep it at a low simmer.

Heat a tablespoon each of the olive oil and butter in a heavy pan and start the onion and garlic cooking in it. After five minutes or so, stir the rice into the onion and cook it gently for a further five minutes or more, stirring often to avoid burning the rice. This seals the individual grains and controls the amount of starch leaked, critical in distinguishing risotto from porridge. Now turn up the heat and pour in the wine, stirring all the time until it has evaporated. Turn the heat down again and pour in a ladleful of hot stock, about 150mls – use a soup ladle, a big cup or a small jug; what you need is just enough liquid to keep the rice simmering, without drowning it or stopping the cooking. In effect, the rice is braising rather than simmering, I suppose. Stir it often and gently until the liquid is almost completely absorbed, then add another measure of stock, and so on.

Check individual grains of rice regularly once about two thirds of the stock has been used, because it's impossible to predict exactly how much liquid the rice will absorb. The rice is done when the grains are cooked through but retain some firmness. The liquid should be almost totally absorbed and the risotto slightly creamy from released starch. The process should take about 20 minutes from the time you put in the wine, but start checking grains much earlier than that.

When you put in what you expect to be the final ladle of stock, chop the asparagus and mangetout and stir them and the pinenuts in too. The mangetout will cook just a little, but that's as much as it likes to be cooked anyway. When the liquid is all but gone, take the risotto off the heat and gently stir in the remaining butter and olive oil, the parmesan, any fresh herbs you're using, and plenty of salt and pepper.

Serve a mound of risotto and a few roasted beetroots on each of four warmed plates and drizzle some basil oil around. Offer more parmesan to be sprinkled or shaved over the risotto. And say a prayer for Irish tourists everywhere facing their first soggy risotto today.

Watercress and red onion risotto

with pan-fried mushrooms

I love the pungency of vibrantly fresh watercress and would rarely cook it at all, saving it instead for salads. That's why in this recipe the watercress is added at the end; if you want to soften its flavour, add the watercress with the last ladle of stock instead. The same reasoning applies to the red onions, which are here as featured vegetables, not in the usual background oniony way, which is why they are cooked separately. It would be very difficult not to overcook them if they were done in the same pan as the risotto. I use oyster mushrooms, not only because I get brilliant ones delivered from Forest Mushrooms in North Cork but also because of their subtle flavour and their quick and easy cooking. If you use other mushrooms, especially field or flat ones, they may leak a lot more juice, not necessarily a bad thing.

FOR FOUR:

- 60g butter
- 60mls olive oil
- 6 small red onions, sliced in half-rounds
- 100g watercress
- 6 cloves of garlic, chopped
- 1200mls stock
- 320g arborio or other risotto rice
- 120mls dry white wine
- 60g fresh parmesan, grated
- salt and pepper

- 150g fresh oyster mushrooms, whole or halved
- 2 tblspns butter
- small handful parsley, chopped

IN A SMALL PAN, warm half a tablespoon each of the butter and olive oil and stew all but one of the onions in it, gently and stirring occasionally, until the onions have become tender and sweeter, but not soft. Wash the watercress, tear the leaves and chop the stalks fairly small. Meanwhile, start the risotto.

Heat a tablespoon each of the olive oil and butter in a heavy pan and start the garlic and one of the onions cooking in it. In another pot, keep the stock barely simmering. After five minutes or so, stir the rice into the onion and cook it gently for a further five to ten minutes. Now turn up the heat and pour in the wine, stirring all the time until it has evaporated. Turn the heat back down and pour in a ladleful of hot stock; what you need is just enough to keep the rice simmering, without drowning it or stopping the cooking. Stir it often and gently until the liquid is almost completely absorbed, then add another measure of stock, and so on.

Check individual grains of rice regularly once about two thirds of the stock has been used. The rice is done when it is cooked through but retains some firmness. The liquid should be totally absorbed and the risotto slightly creamy. This should take about 20 minutes. When the liquid is all but gone, take the risotto off the heat and gently stir in the watercress and onions, the remaining butter and olive oil, the parmesan, and plenty of salt and pepper.

Cook the mushrooms as the risotto is finishing, they will only take five minutes or so. Melt a tablespoon of butter in a frying pan, fry the mushrooms fairly briskly, turning them once or twice. Just as they appear to be done, add in the other tablespoon of butter, the parsley and a good seasoning of salt and pepper, and take the pan off the heat immediately.

Serve the mushrooms and the risotto, pouring the pan juices over them.

Radicchio and roasted pumpkin risotto

with gingered pumpkin cream and braised fennel

Pumpkin risotto is my ultimate comfort food and the gingered pumpkin cream here adds another layer of pampering for pumpkin lovers. I must admit I first made the cream for its colour and was a bit insecure about the whole dish, which also featured braised beetroot and leek along with the fennel; it looked stunning. Anyway, some of the fussiest of risotto eaters gave it the all-clear and I relaxed. The radicchio's function in this bliss zone is to give a slightly bitter contrasting edge, though it loses a lot of its bitterness in the brief cooking it gets here. As often as not, when I want the dish to be its pure comforting self, I would leave it out or replace it with a less challenging green like chard or black kale. If you go for the whole package and serve the braised fennel here, start it first and check it often. The cooking time can vary wildly, depending on the age of the fennel amongst other things, but it will happily sit waiting in a low oven.

FOR FOUR:

- 400g pumpkin flesh
- 1 dstspn grated ginger
- 300mls stock or water
- 100mls single cream
- 1 small head of radicchio
- 60mls olive oil
- 60g butter
- 1 onion, chopped
- 6 cloves of garlic, chopped
- 1200mls stock
- 320g arborio or other risotto rice
- 120mls dry white wine
- 60g fresh parmesan, grated
- salt and pepper
- braised fennel (see page 24)

YOU'LL NEED A PUMPKIN of about 800g to get 400g of useful flesh. Chop the flesh into small bite-size pieces. Toss 300g of these with some olive oil and butter in an oven tray and roast them in a moderate oven, stirring them occasionally, until they are tender.

Put the rest of the pumpkin in a small pan with the ginger and 300mls of stock, and simmer it gently until the pumpkin has broken down into the liquid, then blend this to a fine puree. Add the cream, a little salt and a pinch of cayenne pepper, maybe, and simmer again until the sauce has reduced and thickened. I like to serve a small, intense amount of the cream rather than a thin pool of it. It's probably best to leave this last stage until the risotto is almost finished.

To cook the radicchio, tear the leaves coarsely, heat some olive oil in a pan, toss in the leaves and stir them over a high heat until they wilt. This will only take a minute, so do it during the cooking of the risotto.

Cook the basic risotto (see page 112). When you put in what you have judged to be the last measure of liquid, stir in the roasted pumpkin and radicchio as well. When the last of the liquid has been absorbed, stir in the remaining olive oil and butter, and the grated parmesan and season the risotto generously. Serve a mound of risotto on each of four warm plates and pour a stream of the pumpkin cream around it. Arrange a few pieces of braised fennel on each plate and offer extra parmesan to be sprinkled over the risotto.

Roasted roots and couscous pilaff

with harissa-sweet pepper oil and pastries or felafel

The intensified sweetness of the roots and the mingled flavours of the chermoula and herbs make this pilaff one of those things you can't stop eating. The hot and sweet oil adds a touch of excitement, but to really do the pilaff proud, serve it surrounded with a variety of small intensely flavoured snacks - some that I use are tiny filo pastry parcels of feta cheese, deep-fried felafel and aubergine-chilli rolls. The reason I do the pilaff with roots is simply to give the roots their big day out - everybody looks down on the poor things - but as the year wears on you can add any other roasted vegetable (asparagus, beans, peppers and courgettes work well) but roast them separately from the roots and add them in with the couscous. By the way, the weight given for the roots is for the amount you need after peeling, coring etc.

FOR FOUR:

- 600g root vegetables – carrots, swede turnips, parsnips, celeriac
- 1 dstspn cumin seeds
- 1 dstspn fennel seeds
- 6 cloves of garlic, peeled and halved
- 2 red onions, coarsely chopped
- salt and pepper
- olive oil
- 320g couscous
- 300mls stock or water
- about 100mls chermoula (see page 35)
- fresh coriander
- fresh parsley
- 200mls harissa-sweet pepper oil (see page 34)

PEEL THE ROOTS, cut the woody cores out of the parsnips, then chop the roots into large bite-size pieces, allowing for a small degree of shrinking in the oven. In a pot of boiling water, cook the carrots and turnips for two minutes, then add the other roots and cook for two minutes more. Strain the vegetables, and toss them in a roasting dish with the seeds, garlic and the onion. Season with salt and pepper, stir in enough olive oil to coat the vegetables, and put the dish in a fairly hot oven, 350–380°F (Gas Mark 4–5). The vegetables will need to be tossed and turned once or twice during cooking, which should take 20–30 minutes. Keep an eye on the oven temperature – the vegetables should brown and caramelize a little at the edges, but serious browning before being cooked means the oven is too hot; too low a temperature will cook the vegetables in a sweaty way, without any delicious caramelizing.

Meanwhile, cook the couscous by pouring 300mls of hot water or light stock over the 320g of it. Quickly stir it once or twice and leave it to soak for 15 minutes. Sift it with a fork, slotted spoon or, most efficiently, your fingers. Stir the couscous into the vegetables, sprinkle a few splashes of water over, cover the dish with foil, and return it to the oven to heat through (five or ten minutes). Just before serving, stir in the chermoula and handfuls of chopped fresh coriander and parsley, if you've got them handy. This won't cool the pilaff unduly; it tastes best a good few degrees down from hot anyway.

Spoon mounds of the pilaff on to four plates and pour a stream of the harissa-sweet pepper oil around each. Leave a jug of extra oil on the table, or a little straight harissa, for the chilli fiends among you.

Penne with fennel, green peppers, olives
and roasted garlic-parsley oil

While I would generally go along with the idea that the best thing to go with pasta is whatever you've got in the cupboard, a bottle of wine and an appetite, this is one of those specific recipes. I've tried (and eaten happily) other vegetables with this sauce, but there is no denying that this lot were made for each other. The recipe for the garlic-parsley oil makes about 500mls, enough for at least ten people, but it's hard to make less unless you've got miniature kitchen equipment. It will keep well in the fridge for a week or so.

FOR FOUR:

- 16 cloves garlic
- 300mls olive oil
- 2 large handfuls, about 80–100g, parsley
- salt and pepper

- 450g dried penne pasta
- 1 fennel bulb
- 2 green peppers
- 12–16 black olives, stoned and halved

FIRST MAKE THE OIL. Make two or more times the recipe if you've got the ingredients. Separate the garlic cloves from each other, toss them in a little olive oil and roast them in a low to moderate oven until they are soft and lightly browned. The garlic should now be easy to squeeze from its skin. Put it in a food processor with the parsley and blend to a fairly fine pulp. Pour in the olive oil and blend to get an oil of slightly thick pouring consistency. Season with salt and pepper.

Boil a large pot of water for the pasta, then start cooking the vegetables. Cut the fennel in half lengthways, then again into quarters. Chop these pieces crossways into thin slices. In a heavy pan, warm a little olive oil and cook the fennel gently for about five minutes, then chop the green pepper in the same way and add it to the pan. Continue cooking gently, stirring often, for another five minutes until the vegetables are tender but not soft. Add the olives and cook for just one minute more. Meanwhile cook the pasta in the water, drain it and return it to the pot. Stir in the vegetables and four tablespoons of the garlic-parsley oil and warm it through. Before serving, test for seasoning and flavour, you may want to add more of the oil. A hard, mature sheep's cheese, grated or shaved, is brilliant with this, though parmesan is more than good enough.

Pasta ribbons in lemon sauce

with spinach, leeks and tomatoes

I'm not being coy here but, honestly, I can't remember where I first saw the idea of pasta with lemon, a cross-breed of comfort food and refreshment. The combination of vegetables in this version isn't sacred but I wouldn't stray far from the essential mix of fresh greens, mild onions and sweet dried tomatoes. Some puy lentils are excellent in it but you would need to be sure you want to add such an earthy element to an otherwise light and heady mix. I've given quantities for two people for this dish because of the type of pasta used. While it is as easy to make a cauldron for twelve as a pan for two of pasta, vegetables and oil using dried short pasta pieces like penne or macaroni, the same cannot be said of fresh long ribbons or noodles, especially with a cream sauce. The pasta absorbs all the sauce and becomes flaccid before you can thoroughly stir it in, then it sticks to the pan, then one person gets all the tomatoes while someone else gets soggy pasta and the onions. So, should you never cook fresh pasta for more than two? No, it's not impossible, but you need a slightly different approach. When the pasta is cooked, drain it and put it straight on to warm plates, share out the sauce over the noodles and combine each portion with a few deft flicks of a pair of tongs or forks.

FOR TWO:

- 2 handfuls of fresh spinach
- ½ lemon, rind and juice
- 2 cloves garlic, finely chopped
- 80mls white wine
- 1 small leek, thinly sliced in rounds
- 2 sundried tomatoes (ie 4 halves), thinly sliced
- 250g fresh pasta ribbons, tagliatelle, fettuccine, papperdelle etc.
- 200mls single cream
- salt and pepper

DROP THE SPINACH into boiling water, leave it for a minute then plunge it into cold water. Squeeze it to remove most of the water, chop it and set it aside while you get on with the sauce.

Put the lemon, garlic, wine, a half glass of water and the leeks into a small pan, bring to the boil and simmer gently for six to eight minutes, until the leek has softened a little, then add the tomatoes and remove the pan from the heat.

Meanwhile, boil enough water to accommodate the pasta comfortably, add a little oil, then slide in the pasta. Cook the pasta at a rolling boil, stir it occasionally and test it often. Fresh pasta can cook in anything from three to eight minutes, and it can go from cooked to flabbily overcooked while you're trying to remember where you left your wine glass. When it's as cooked as you like it, drain it and return it to the pan.

Just before you drain the pasta, pour the cream into the sauce, bring it back to the boil and simmer for a minute. It should thicken a little but still be a very thin cream. Add this sauce and the spinach to the pasta pan, season generously, stir to combine everything quickly, then divide the dish between two warmed plates. Serve with some recently grated parmesan or crumbled goat's cheese; a little fresh parsley, basil or fennel, either in the sauce or scattered over the finished dish, will add an extra dimension.

Pasta in basil oil

with aubergines, broad beans, red onions and chillies

There has been one version or another of this dish on Paradiso menus for most of the restaurant's life. It is, I think, a kind of pre-planned 'pasta with whatever's in the fridge' dish. At one time or another, just about every vegetable in the store has had a night out with the basil oil and some pasta. This recipe is one of my own favourite combinations. I think I could eat pasta with aubergines, chillies and olive oil for the rest of my life and you'd hardly hear so much as a whimper of a moan from me. For the most part, the vegetables are cooked separately and brought together in the basil oil as it gently heats up. This gives the dish the sense of being a collection of happily met individual flavours and textures, rather than one where the separate elements have spent a long time together and melted to form one complex flavour. Not that there's anything wrong with that, I like soup too. The quantities depend on what you've got to hand and whether you like your pasta smothered or in the fashionably austere 'authentic' way. I happen to like it both ways and, I'm told, tend to serve it somewhere in between. I do know that I use a lot of oil, about two tablespoons per person, as a sauce. Some people carefully leave it behind while others mop it up with their fingers. Use as much as you want to eat and watch to learn how others like it. You can learn a lot about people this way. If you don't have a herb-flavoured oil to hand, use a good olive oil and whatever suitable herbs you do have. Parsley, oregano, marjoram, rosemary or thyme aren't bad substitutes. Don't use a cheap or flavourless oil as there's no point in eating lots of tasteless fat. Presuming that the chillies are fairly mild, this quantity will frighten nobody and you can adjust it by leaving out some or all of the seeds. Two tiny 'bird's eye' chillies per person is a perfect medium voltage hit that allows all the other flavours to shine through.

FOR FOUR:

- 1 small aubergine
- a little olive oil
- 2 handfuls of broad beans
- 450g pasta, any shape, fresh or dried
- 120mls basil oil (see page 39)
- 2 small red onions, sliced in thinnish half-rounds
- 4 cloves garlic, sliced
- 2 large fresh chillies, thinly sliced or 8 chopped dried 'bird's eye'
- 1 tomato, deseeded, halved and sliced
- ½ tsp salt

SLICE THE AUBERGINE into 10cm-thick rounds, brush them on both sides with olive oil and roast them in a moderate-hot oven until they are soft and lightly browned. Chop the rounds into halves or quarters and set them aside.

Cook the broad beans in boiling water until tender, six to eight minutes if you're using fresh; whatever the pack says, if frozen. Drain the beans and keep them with the aubergine pieces.

Bring a large pot of water to a boil and cook the pasta in it, stirring and testing it often until it is done to your liking, then drain the pasta and return it to the pot. While the pasta is cooking, put a couple of tablespoons of the oil in a smaller pan and gently cook the onions, garlic and chilli for a few minutes. You want the onions to soften a little but not to break down and become a background flavour. Now add in the rest of the oil, the aubergine pieces and broad beans, the tomato and salt. Gently warm it through and, when you have drained the pasta and returned it to its pot, stir the vegetables and oil into the pasta. Rinse the vegetable pan with a splash of water and tip this into the pasta pot too. It will help, as you gently reheat the pasta, to prevent it from getting fried or sticking to the pot. Check the seasoning and stir in any fresh herbs you want to use, then serve the pasta on to the waiting four warmed plates. As always, offer recently grated parmesan or a lump of it to be shaved at the table.

Moroccan-spiced vegetable and almond pastries with a cucumber-coriander yoghurt sauce

It is what I think of as the 'sweet' spices in these pastries that prompt me to call them Moroccan-spiced. Maybe these spices trigger memories in me of a trip through Morocco long ago, maybe it was something I read in a book. The only pastry I remember from that teenage holiday was eaten on the rooftop of a posh hotel and claimed to feature pigeon. Forgive me, I was young and curious. This humbler version features mostly root vegetables because they are best suited to carrying these spices. We use small oval oven dishes, 10cm long, 7cm wide and 2cm high, to bake one generous pastry per person. The advantage of using a dish is in being able to form sides on the pastry capable of holding themselves up, and getting a smooth finish on top with the seams underneath. However, the filing is the important thing and it will be perfectly happy if the pastry is simply wrapped around it, in any shape or size, and baked. One large pie from which you slice wedges would be the next best thing. As well as the cucumber-yoghurt sauce, I would serve some couscous and something fiery hot, like chickpeas with fresh chillies. Use a thick, rich yoghurt as the cucumber will dilute it considerably. You want a thick pouring sauce, not a thin watery mess.

FOR FOUR:

- 400g roots – carrots, turnips, parsnips, celeriac – at least two types
- 200g green beans
- 2 onions, finely chopped
- 6 garlic cloves, finely chopped
- 2 tsps whole black mustard seeds
- ½ tsp chopped dried chillies
- 1 tsp fennel seeds, ground
- 6 cloves, ground
- 2 tsps coriander seeds, ground
- 1 whole star anise, ground
- ¼ tsp cinnamon
- ½ tsp nutmeg
- ½ tsp turmeric
- 100mls single cream
- ½ tsp salt
- rind of 1 orange
- 80g whole almonds, toasted and chopped
- 1 egg yolk
- 12 sheets filo pastry
- 80g melted butter

- ½ medium cucumber
- 1 clove garlic
- 300mls yoghurt
- small handful fresh coriander, chopped
- ½ tsp salt
- pinch of cayenne pepper

CHOP THE ROOTS INTO SMALL DICE and cook them in boiling water for a few minutes until just tender. Do the same with the green beans and mix them with the cooked roots in a bowl. Fry the onion and garlic in a little oil with the mustard seeds and the chilli. Add the other spices when the onion is cooked, and fry for a minute more. Pour in the cream, add the salt and orange rind, bring it to the boil and simmer for half a minute to thicken the cream. Stir this spiced cream into the vegetables and leave it to cool before adding the almonds and the egg yolk.

Preheat the oven to 350°F (Gas Mark 4). Lay four sheets of pastry on a worktop, brush them with melted butter, lay another sheet on top of each, brush again with butter, then lay a third sheet on each. Now cut the layered pastry into strips the width of the base of the oven dishes you're using, and long enough to line the base of the dish and fold over fully on top. Three strips per oven dish is good, four is better. Brush the dishes with butter and lay one pastry strip in the base of each, overhanging evenly at both ends. Lay the next strip over the first and angled across it, overhanging in the same way. Use the third strip, and a fourth if you've got it, in the same way to completely cover the base and sides of the dish. Spoon in enough of the vegetables to almost fill the dish, then fold over the overhanging strips of pastry to fully cover the top. Tuck in or cut off any excess, then brush the tops with butter.

Bake the pastries at about 350°F (Gas Mark 4) for ten minutes, check that the pastry has firmed up at the sides and has become loose from the ramekin. If it has, carefully flip each one over on to an oven tray lined with baking parchment and remove the ramekin. Return the pastries to the oven, uncovered, and bake for a further ten minutes or so, until the pastry is crisp and lightly browned.

While the pastries are cooking, or a few hours earlier if you prefer, make the cucumber sauce. Peel the cucumber and use a teaspoon to scoop out the seeds. Coarsely chop the cucumber and put it in a food processor with the garlic. Blend to a coarse puree, add the yoghurt and coriander and blend again for a few seconds, then put it in a bowl and season with salt and a tiny pinch of cayenne pepper.

Pumpkin, almond and spring cabbage dolma in a feta custard, with coriander pesto

Strictly speaking, spring cabbage and pumpkin wouldn't see much of each other in the course of a year, the last of well-stored pumpkins just about meeting the first of the spring cabbages. But the thin, dark, supple leaves of spring cabbage are the best wrappers for this dish, so I'm giving you this version. I've used savoy (a bit too chunky), spinach and chard (fine, a bit delicate and hard to get enough leaves big enough) and even kale (emergencies only). I wasn't too convinced about the feta custard the first time I used it, but now I really like the fact that the feta is outside the dolma and falling off them, making it a peripheral, background flavour, something feta rarely is, leaving the pumpkin to shine through. I would serve a couscous and vegetable pilaff with this, or simply buttered couscous and some chilli-spiced chickpeas or green beans.

FOR FOUR:

- 500g pumpkin flesh
- 1 onion
- 2 cloves garlic
- 1 dstspn cumin seeds
- 1 small chilli
- ¼ tsp salt
- ¼ tsp nutmeg
- ¼ tsp cinnamon
- fresh coriander
- 80g whole almonds, lightly roasted
- 1 egg yolk
- 12 leaves of spring cabbage

- 120g feta cheese
- 1 egg
- 320mls plain yoghurt
- 1 clove of garlic
- pinch of cayenne pepper

- 4–6 tblspns coriander-chilli pesto (see page 38)

TO GET 500g OF PUMPKIN FLESH, you will need to peel and deseed a pumpkin of 1–1.5kg. Chop the flesh coarsely, steam it until just cooked, and mash it roughly – don't use a food processor or blender. Finely chop the onion, garlic and chilli, and cook them in a little oil with the cumin seeds until the onions are soft. Stir this into the pumpkin and add the salt and the other herbs and spices. Coarsely chop the almonds, by hand or carefully in a food processor, and add these in too. Add the egg yolk when the mixture has cooled. Just before you fill the leaves, check the consistency of the filling – if it seems too wet and soft stir in some ground almonds, breadcrumbs or raw couscous, and wait another ten minutes.

Trim the cabbage leaves, shaving any thick stalks down to the thickness of the leaf, then drop the leaves into boiling water for about five minutes. Rinse in cold water and drain off the water.

To make the custard, simply blend the cheese, egg, yoghurt, garlic and cayenne in a food processor.

Place about a tablespoon of pumpkin mash at the base of each cabbage leaf, roll the leaf up half a turn, tuck in the sides, and continue to roll the leaf all the way up. Keep a little pressure on as you roll, to get a fairly tight parcel, and trim the top of the leaf to finish with a neat edge at the end. Arrange the parcels close together in an oiled oven dish, the neat edges on the bottom, and pour the custard over the top – it should seep down a little but sit on top too, to prevent the dolma burning. Bake in a moderate oven, 300–350°F (Gas Mark 2–4), for 30–40 minutes, until the custard is lightly browned and softly set, not dried up.

Serve three dolma per person, with some of the custard clinging to them, and the coriander-chilli pesto drizzled over.

Couscous-crusted aubergine,

pan-fried, with an almond, chilli and scallion filling, sweet pepper concasse and spinach with chickpeas, lemon and cumin

This is the big aubergine dish on the summer menu as I write. There's always a striking aubergine dish and they're usually successful, but this one takes the biscuit. If poor Tamzin has to trim and roast one more aubergine we'll lose her ... oops, there she goes. I was very tempted to try and make up a new version of this recipe to disguise the fact that it gets its inside colour and a special part of its flavour from sambal oelek, a commercial Indonesian chilli sauce and one of my favourite tastes. But here, opposite, is the truth of the matter. If you can, try a few different brands, they have varying chilli-heat levels and other flavours. I have a preference for one with a distinctly sweet and medium-hot taste, and that is what this aubergine dish should have. The chilli shouldn't mask the other subtler flavours of the almonds, the scallions or the aubergine itself.

FOR FOUR:

- 4 medium aubergines
- 4 scallions
- 2 cloves of garlic
- a little olive oil
- 80g cream cheese
- 100g whole almonds, lightly toasted and finely chopped
- 2 tsps sambal oelek
- 1 tblspn chermoula (see page 35)
- 300g cooked couscous
- 50g flour
- 1 egg
- 100mls milk

- 2 yellow peppers
- 2 tomatoes, seeded
- 1 red onion
- 2 cloves of garlic
- salt and pepper
- approx. 100mls olive oil

- 4 large handfuls of spinach
- 1 red onion, thinly sliced
- rind and juice of ½ lemon
- 2 tsps cumin seeds
- 4 tblspns of cooked chickpeas

TRIM THE AUBERGINES by cutting thin slices lengthways off opposite sides. Now cut the remaining piece of aubergine in two. If the aubergines are fat, you may get three slices from each one – each slice should be about 15mm thick. Brush both sides of each slice with olive oil and roast at about 350°F (Gas Mark 4) in an oven until lightly browned and cooked through.

Meanwhile, chop the scallions into thin rings and fry them with the garlic in a little olive oil for half a minute, no more. Mash the cream cheese, by hand or in a food processor, then stir in the almonds, scallions and the sambal oelek – it should have a thick, spreadable consistency. Spread a generous layer on an aubergine slice, put a matching slice on top, and repeat with the rest of the aubergine slices.

Stir the chermoula into the couscous and put it in a wide dish. Coat the filled aubergines by tossing them in flour, dunking them in the egg-milk mix and, finally, tossing them in the couscous. Make sure they are well coated. If you have time, put the finished aubergines in the fridge for a little while to firm up again.

Chop the peppers and tomato into small dice, finely chop the onion and garlic, and put the lot in a small pan. Add seasoning and enough olive oil to just come up to the top. If your peppers are merely yellow and not summer-sweet, add a large pinch of sugar and a splash of balsamic vinegar. Place the pan over a very low heat and allow to heat through slowly for about ten minutes – it's best if the vegetables cook a little while the oil never quite boils.

Prepare the ingredients for the spinach before you start to fry the aubergines. Tear the leaves into pieces. Put the rind and juice of the lemon in a jug and add an equal quantity of water.

Fry the aubergines at a fairly high temperature, in enough cooking oil to come halfway up their sides, turning them once or twice, until they are crisped and lightly browned. Keep them warm in the oven while you cook the spinach. Heat some olive oil to quite hot in a pan large enough to take the volume of raw spinach, and cook the onion in it for half a minute, then add the cumin, chickpeas and spinach. Keep stirring over a high heat as the spinach wilts. When the spinach seems almost cooked, tip in the lemon and some seasoning and stir for a few seconds more to allow the water to boil off. About two minutes is all it should take.

Place a pile of spinach and a fried aubergine on each plate, and spoon some of the concasse, including the liquid, over the aubergines.

Thai tofu-cashew fritters

with pineapple chutney and coconut-stewed vegetables

I put these fritters on the first Café Paradiso dinner menu in an attempt to do something with tofu other than chopping and frying it. There were a few other tofu experiments before we opened, the worst of which was optimistically marinating it in something other than soya sauce to change the context to something European. We tried a red wine-based marinade, then threw the lot away. Anyway the fritters became a favourite with the staff and the customers, and I came to see it as the foundation rock of the menu. The dish has survived umpteen seasonal menu changes and I don't think it will ever go away now. When coating the fritters, you might find the classic egg-milk combination more efficient than the water in these instructions. We only do it this way to leave the dish fully vegan. For the vegetable stew, you can use any vegetables you've got to hand. I tend to stick to a simple combination of roots and greens; say turnips, carrots, cabbage and green beans – four is enough, any more can become too confusing. Avoid sweet vegetables like peppers, they're not good with the already sweet coconut sauce.

FOR FOUR:

- 2 x 200g blocks of firm tofu
- 300mls shoyu
- 100mls water
- 4 cloves of garlic, halved
- 1 x 4cm piece ginger, sliced
- 1 tsp tomato puree
- juice of ½ lemon

FOR THE FILLING:

- 150g cashews
- large pinch of cayenne pepper
- 1 tsp ground cumin seeds
- 1 tsp ground coriander seeds
- 100mls hot water

TO FINISH:

- 100g flour
- 200g coarse maize
- water
- oil for shallow frying

SLICE THE TOFU into twenty-four equal pieces about 30mm x 40mm and 5mm thick. Dilute the shoyu with the water and stir in the crushed garlic, the ginger, tomato and lemon juice. Place the tofu slices into this marinade and leave it for at least two hours or overnight.

Lightly toast the cashews, then grind them with the spices in a food processor. With the motor still running, gradually pour in the water to get a thick puree. Be careful, you may not need all the water.

Take the tofu from the marinade. Don't throw away the marinade – either slip another block of tofu into it or use it as a seasoning like soya sauce in stir fries, rice dishes and the like. Spread a layer of cashew puree between two slices of tofu and repeat with the rest of the tofu to get twelve small sandwiches. Put the flour in a shallow tray or dish and toss the sandwiches in it, making sure they are well coated. Put the coarse maize in another tray and half fill a small bowl with water. Taking one or two of the sandwiches at a time, quickly dunk them in the water and then toss them in the maize to completely coat them.

When you are ready to serve, heat the oil in a large frying pan and fry the sandwiches over a fairly high heat for a few minutes on each side. You'll need to do them in two batches, but they will keep well in a warm oven.

FOR THE VEGETABLE STEW:

- 1 onion
- 4 cloves of garlic, chopped
- 1 tblspn grated ginger
- 2 dried chillies, ground
- 2 tsps coriander seeds, ground
- 4 ripe tomatoes, chopped
- 150g creamed coconut
- rind and juice of 1 lime
- 1 tsp salt
- 600mls water
- 600g vegetables – carrots, green beans, cabbage, swede turnips
- fresh coriander leaves

SLICE THE ONION INTO THIN QUARTER rounds and cook in a little oil in a large pan for five minutes. Add the garlic, ginger, chilli and coriander and cook until the onion has softened. Now add the tomatoes and stew them until they begin to break down. Coarsely chop the coconut block and add it in with the lime, salt and water. Bring the sauce to a boil, stirring to help melt in the coconut, then turn down the heat and simmer the sauce for ten minutes.

Meanwhile, chop the carrots and turnips into large-bite chunks and boil or steam them together until they are just tender. Chop the cabbage leaves into similar-sized pieces and cook them with the green beans until just done also, then mix all the vegetables together.

Add the vegetables to the coconut sauce and continue to simmer for a further ten minutes. I like the stew to be quite dry and rich, so after ten minutes simmering I increase the temperature to boil off most, but not all, of the water. Stir in lots of chopped fresh coriander at the end.

Serve the fritters with the stew, the pineapple chutney on page 34, and the fragrant rice on page 29.

Pistachio, green chilli and yoghurt kofta

with kale in a fresh tomato-coconut sauce and cardamom-lime pancakes

This is one of many different kofta dishes we've been doing since I first took a shine to a simple basic recipe in a book by Tarla Dalal. The basic combination of yoghurt, gram flour and spices is essentially a dumpling batter which, when deep-fried, is delicious on its own in a sauce but will also accommodate all kinds of additions – different nuts & spices, chopped cooked vegetables like aubergine, peppers, roots or mashed pumpkin. The tomato-coconut sauce is so more-ish in its own right that we usually serve the kofta in soup-like portions of it and use spoons to slurp what the kofta and pancakes don't absorb. Although the kofta are ideally suited to being part of an Indian feast including breads, rice, chutneys, curries, dhals and so on, it would be a rare occasion when we would undertake the preparation required. A small portion can make a stimulating starter, but most often we serve them at lunch as they are here, nestling with a little greenery in a rich soup with some simple pancakes for mopping up. The quantities here are for a bare four portions with no leftovers. However, everything keeps well and its no more trouble to make it up to six or more. I would recommend you make as much sauce as you've got tomatoes, as many pancakes as you can be bothered and only as much kofta batter as you will need today.

FOR FOUR:

- 200mls thick yoghurt
- 100g gram flour
- 50g shelled pistachios
- 2 fresh green chillies
- 1 tsp cumin seeds
- ½ tsp turmeric
- ¼ tsp salt
- small handful of fresh coriander, chopped
- ¼ tsp bicarbonate of soda
- 4–5 stalks of kale, to serve

FOR THE SAUCE:

- 1 onion, finely chopped
- 2 cloves of garlic, chopped
- 2 tsp grated ginger
- 1 tsp medium curry powder
- 400g ripe tomatoes, chopped
- 50g coconut cream block
- 400mls water
- 30mls single cream
- ¼ tsp salt

PUT THE YOGHURT in a bowl and sift the gram flour over it. Chop the pistachios and add them to the bowl. Slice the chillies in half lengthways, then chop them into thin half-rounds and add these to the bowl with the cumin seeds, turmeric, salt and coriander. Stir everything together to get a thick batter – add the soda just before you begin deep-frying the kofta.

Cook the onion in a little oil for a few minutes, then add the garlic and spices and continue cooking until the onion is soft. Add the tomatoes and stew them until they break down, then add the coconut and the water. Simmer for ten minutes, then puree the sauce, sieve out the solids and return the liquid to the pan. Add the cream and boil briskly for one minute. The consistency should be that of a thin creamy soup, which is what it is really, I suppose. Keep it warm, or set it aside to be reheated as you need it.

Deep-fry the kofta by carefully sliding teaspoonfuls into hot oil, preferably at about 180°C/350°F, in batches. Cook them until golden brown, turning them once. Keep batches warm in an oven while you cook the rest. At the same time, take the kale off the stalks, coarsely chop it and cook it in boiling water for a few minutes. Ladle the sauce into bowls, put six or seven kofta in each one and tuck little bunches of kale in around them. Scatter some fresh coriander over each bowl and serve with a pile of warm pancakes.

FOR 12–16 CARDAMOM-LIME PANCAKES:

- 20 cardamom seeds
- 60g strong flour
- 60g rice flour
- ¼ tsp salt
- rind and juice ½ lime
- 1 egg
- 240mls coconut milk

TAKE THE BLACK SEEDS from the cardamom pods and discard the pods. Crush the seeds in a grinder. Sift the flours, salt, lime rind and cardamom. Whisk the egg into the coconut milk and the lime juice, then whisk this into the flours. This should give you a thick pouring batter. Heat a large frying pan to a medium-low heat. Brush it very lightly with oil, then pour in one to three small ladlefuls of the batter, about one tablespoon each to give a diameter of about 5cm. Fry the pancakes for about two minutes, then flip them over and fry the other side. Turn them out on to a plate in a random pile – they won't stick to each other. If you make them in advance, and you can – up to a day – they reheat very well in a low oven.

Aubergine gamelastra

with a roasted pepper sauce, puy lentils and polenta croutons

This was the first dish of mine that I really loved and felt was my own creation. It's full of earthy, intense flavours balanced with the sunny lightness of red peppers, polenta and sundried tomatoes; and then, at the end of the day, it's serene and comforting too. The name relates not to the ingredients, cooking style or nationality, but to the fact that I was thinking about the extraordinary first public airing of the Cork University's Gamelan orchestra, for which we did some interpretations of Indonesian food. This dish has nothing to do with it other than that I know it wouldn't have happened without it, if you know what I mean. The pepper sauce recipe has been around and will make enough for six or more, but it is hard to make less and it is almost certainly too delicious to last very long.

FOR FOUR:

- 4 small-medium aubergines
- a little olive oil
- 150g kale
- 70g stilton, crumbled
- 2 sundried tomatoes, finely chopped
- 40g breadcrumbs
- 1 onion, finely chopped
- 4 cloves garlic, finely chopped
- 1 tsp mustard, Dijon style
- 30mls single cream

FOR THE PEPPER SAUCE:

- 2 red peppers
- 2 cloves garlic, chopped
- 200mls light stock or water
- 100mls single cream
- pinch of cayenne pepper
- ½ tsp salt

- polenta (see page 41)

- puy lentils, (see page 25)

If you are serving the polenta croutons with this, you will need to make the polenta at least an hour before you need it, though you will only need about a third of the recipe on page 41.

Trim the ends of the aubergines and cut a thin slice off two sides to give a near full-length smooth edge, then cut each aubergine into two thick slices lengthways. If the aubergines seem too big, cut three slices from each one. The slices will need to be at least 15mm thick. Brush both sides of each slice with olive oil and roast them on a tray in a moderate to hot oven, until lightly browned.

Cook the kale by dropping it into boiling water for about three to five minutes, depending on its coarseness. Drain and rinse it immediately in cold water, pressing out as much water as possible. Chop it roughly and put it in a mixing bowl with the stilton, sundried tomatoes and crumbs.

Gently cook the onion and garlic in a little olive oil until softened, then add the mustard and cream and bring to a quick boil before removing from the heat. Cool this a little before adding to the kale, with some chopped parsley and black pepper. Salt is probably not needed because of the stilton.

To make the sauce, roast and peel the peppers as on page 19, then put them in a small pan with the garlic and the water. Simmer these for five or six minutes, then blend to a fine puree. Return the puree to the pan with the cream and seasoning, bring it to the boil and simmer briskly for one minute, no more. The sauce will reheat easily if you make it in advance, though you may have to thin it a little first.

Take four of the aubergine slices and place a generous amount of the kale mixture gently on top of each, then put the other four slices on the kale. Press down gently.

The gamelastras are now ready to go back in the oven, for a further ten to fifteen minutes, so make sure everything else is ready before you go on. They will happily sit around for a little while. To finish the gamelastras, bake them at 350°F (Gas Mark 4) for ten to fifteen minutes. Just before serving, cut the cooled polenta into cubes of about 15mm and fry them in a generous amount of olive oil in a heavy non-stick or well-seasoned pan until lightly browned and beginning to crisp, about six to eight minutes.

Serve one gamelastra per person, surrounded by a pool of pepper sauce, a pile of polenta croutons and some puy lentils.

Gingered kale, walnut and pumpkin gratin

with lemon-cumin sauce and aubergine-chilli rolls

There is a sense of loss when summer fades away, not just for the sunshine but for its freshly picked, life-enhancing produce; but these two vegetables, kale and pumpkin, and a few others (leeks definitely, roots maybe) almost turn autumn and winter into something to look forward to. This dish has so many of my favourite vegetables and flavours in it I almost fall over with excitement making it for the first time each year. I love the way the combination of gingered kale, mashed pumpkin and lemon cream strays deep into comfort food territory, the texture of walnuts reins it in and the explosive chilli-heat of the aubergine rolls wakes your tastebuds, screaming. I was as surprised as anyone when this dish evolved into this incarnation. I was originally trying to do something clever with mashed potatoes and cabbage or kale. Deconstructed colcannon or some such nonsense. You will need very good pumpkins, deep orange in colour, sweet and with dry, dense flesh. We have an abundant supply, from the heroic Organic Joe in West Cork, of a Japanese variety called Hokaido which usually weighs in at a very manageable size of one to two kilos. Then there are the grey-skinned Crowns from Hollyhill Farm, bigger but even denser and more intensely flavoured. I know you only ever see jokey monstrous pumpkins in the shops for a few days each year, but the real things are out there too. If you can't find them in specialist shops, grow your own, they are extraordinary plants. We use the long-leafed Italian black kale, which also comes from Hollyhill, though the more common curly kale is excellent too, a little lighter in flavour. At Paradiso, we cook individual gratins in steel collars 11cm in diameter by 5cm high. They look stunning, surrounded on the plate by the lemon cream and the aubergine rolls. I have no doubt that this presentation contributes to the reaction the dish gets and the pleasure it gives. That puts the gratin firmly in the category of 'restaurant food' as distinct from home cooking, I suppose, and maybe it will put you off. However, individual is the only way I see them so I'm putting down the recipe that way. If you don't have any steel collars to hand, or you think that kind of thing too fiddly and poncy, put the layers in an oven dish, cook the gratin a little longer and serve it up in portions as neatly scooped out as you can manage. Leaving the cooked gratin to sit for five or ten minutes before slicing it will help.

FOR FOUR:

- 1kg pumpkin flesh
- 25g butter
- 100mls cream
- 1 tsp salt
- ¼ tsp nutmeg
- large pinch of cayenne pepper
- 1 egg yolk
- 1 tblspn chopped fresh coriander
- 1 onion, finely chopped
- 1 tblspn grated ginger
- 2 garlic cloves, chopped
- ½ tsp chopped dried chillies
- 4 tomatoes, chopped
- 50mls red wine
- splash of shoyu
- 1 tsp tomato puree
- 240g kale
- 24 walnut halves, lightly toasted

YOU WILL NEED a pumpkin, or pumpkins, of at least 1.5kg to get 1kg of flesh. Peel the pumpkin, chop it in half and scoop out the seeds. Chop the pumpkin flesh into chunks and boil or steam it until just done, then drain it well. It is important that the cooked pumpkin is as dry as possible so, if you boiled it, put the cooked and drained pumpkin back in the pan over a low heat for a few minutes to evaporate any clinging water. Mash the pumpkin thoroughly or

blend it in a food processor (I think this gives a better result). Melt the butter in a pan, add in the cream, salt, cayenne pepper and nutmeg. When this is warm, add the mashed pumpkin and stir it over a medium heat for about five minutes. This should give you a fluffier, richer mash but also a drier one, which is important if it is to sit on top of the gratin. Leave it to cool before adding the egg yolk and coriander.

Heat some cooking oil in a pan and cook the onion with the ginger, garlic and chilli for a few minutes until the onion is soft. Then add in the tomatoes, wine and shoyu. Use the tomato puree only if the tomatoes are not ripe and, well, tomato-flavoured. Bring this up to the boil and simmer it until the tomatoes have broken down to a rich, thick sauce. If you use tinned tomatoes leave out the juice. Cook the kale in boiling water until just done, drain it, chop it into bite-size pieces and add it to the tomato sauce.

Lightly oil the insides of the rings and place them on baking parchment on oven trays. Put a layer of the gingered kale into each one, slice the walnuts and scatter them over the kale, then put a layer of pumpkin mash on top. Bake for about 20 minutes at about 400°F (Gas Mark 6), until the pumpkin starts to brown. Lift a gratin to a (very close) plate with a slice, run the back of a knife between the gratin and the steel ring and lift the ring off. Pour some lemon-cumin cream around each one, then garnish with the aubergine rolls – three each is perfect but chilli fiends will gobble any spares.

LEMON-CUMIN CREAM, FOR FOUR:

- 300mls light stock
- 1 small onion, quartered
- 2 whole cloves of garlic
- rind of 1 lemon
- 1 tblspn lemon juice
- 200mls single cream
- 2 tsps cumin seeds, toasted and ground
- ½ tsp salt

HEAT THE STOCK in a pan with the onion and garlic cloves and simmer it for ten minutes or so, until it has reduced to 100mls. Discard the vegetables and add in the lemon, cream, cumin and salt. Bring the sauce back to the boil and keep it at a lively simmer for a few minutes until it has the consistency of a slightly thickened pouring cream. You should still have about 200mls of sauce.

12 AUBERGINE-CHILLI ROLLS:

- 2 aubergines
- a little olive oil
- 80g ground almonds
- 60g sambal oelek

TRIM THE SIDES of the aubergines by taking a thin lengthways slice off opposite sides. Now cut fairly thin slices, lengthways again, about 5mm thick – you should get six slices from an average aubergine. Brush both sides of each slice with olive oil and roast them on oven trays until cooked through and very lightly coloured. Stir enough ground almonds into the sambal to make a thick spread. It is not possible to be completely accurate about these measurements – what you need is a spread with a consistency something like soft peanut butter. Use a butter knife to spread a thin layer on each cooked aubergine slice, then roll up the slices. The aubergine rolls need only to be warmed through, so put them in the oven for the last five minutes of the gratins' cooking time, or put them in for the few minutes that you are allowing the gratins to cool before serving.

Roast pumpkin with lemon-hazelnut risotto stuffing, leek and parmesan sauce, and roast parsnips and sweetcorn

Maybe it's a personal thing that I shouldn't talk about, but I find any dish involving roast pumpkin very attractive; this one, however, takes the cake. Hard to believe that something so proudly good-looking came about of necessity. In the restaurant, we do it when we build up a stock of undersized Hokaido pumpkins. It also tends to be a 'leftover risotto' dish, but presuming you don't often have quantities of leftover risotto, I've given quantities for a small amount of risotto. In any case, the risotto needs to be cooled down before you use it. If, in the instructions, it seems that you need to do a lot of things at the same time, give yourself a break by preparing the parsnips beforehand, up to tossing them in butter; and make the leek sauce up to the addition of the cream.

FOR FOUR:

- 2 small pumpkins, 600–800g each
- 400mls vegetable stock
- 1 onion, finely chopped
- 4 cloves garlic, finely chopped
- 20g butter
- 50mls dry white wine
- 120g arborio rice
- 2 tblspns hazelnuts
- rind of 1 lemon
- juice of ½ lemon
- 20g fresh parmesan, grated
- 2 tblspns olive oil
- salt and pepper

- 1 small leek, washed and finely chopped
- 2 cloves garlic, finely chopped
- 20g butter
- 40mls white wine
- 60mls light stock or water
- 150mls single cream
- 40g fresh parmesan, grated
- salt and pepper

HALVE THE PUMPKINS and scoop out the seeds. Bring a pot of water to the boil and cook the pumpkin halves in it until just tender. This should take about ten minutes. Remember that the pumpkins will fall apart easily if overcooked, but will not cook very much more in the oven later, so getting to 'just tender' at this stage is important. If you like, you could use some of this cooking water, with stock added, for the risotto.

Keep the stock at a low simmer while you start the risotto by cooking the onion and garlic in a little of the butter. When the onion has softened, pour in the wine and stir until it has all but evaporated. Now put in a ladle of the stock and allow the rice to simmer in it, with only an occasional stir. When the liquid has almost completely evaporated again, put in a further ladle of stock; continue with this until the rice grains are cooked through but retain some firmness.

While the risotto is cooking, roast the hazelnuts in a low-medium oven, peel them if you like by wrapping them in a teatowel and rubbing them together, then slice or chop them. For such a small quantity, do this by hand – a food processor will give you an uneven mixture of powder and whole nuts.

When you feel the rice is done, stir in the hazelnuts, the lemon rind and juice, parmesan, butter, olive oil and plenty of salt and pepper. Leave the risotto to cool to room temperature before filling the pumpkins. If you use it now, the risotto will be too wet and might simply run out from underneath the inverted pumpkins.

Heat an oven to 400°F (Gas Mark 6). Fill the cavities of the cooked pumpkin halves with the risotto and put them, filled side down, on an oven tray lined with baking parchment. Score the pumpkin skins by cutting shallow lines with a sharp knife, brush skins with olive oil and roast in the oven for about 20 minutes, until the skins become crisp and lightly scorched and the scoring lines have opened a little.

While the pumpkins are cooking, fry the leek and garlic in butter for a few minutes in a small pan, then add in the wine and stock and boil for one minute. Just before you serve the pumpkins, add the

- 500g parsnips
- butter, to coat
- 1 large or 2 smaller whole sweetcorn cobs

cream to the leek pan and boil it for two minutes to get a thickened sauce. Off the heat stir in the grated parmesan which should just about melt into the cream. Season carefully with salt and pepper.

Serve one pumpkin half per person, with a generous ladle of the leek sauce and some roast parsnips and sweetcorn. Some simply cooked green beans or other greens would be a fine accompaniment.

Peel the parsnips and chop them into fairly large pieces, allowing for them to shrink by about a third in the oven. Cook the pieces in boiling water for one minute, then toss them in enough butter to coat them, a teaspoon of honey if you have it, and seasoning. Roast them in a hot oven for about 20 minutes.

Lemon tart with praline ice cream

Desserts

¶ Chocolate-pecan brownie ¶ Rhubarb shortbread ¶ Organic strawberries on a hazelnut pavlova ¶ Iced tiramisu terrine with coffee syrup ¶ Little summer puddings ¶ Blackcurrant fool ¶ Dark and white chocolate mousses ¶ Orange and cardamom bombette ¶ Gooseberry-almond tartlets ¶ Ginger-sautéed pears ¶ White chocolate torte ¶ Baked praline-stuffed peaches

Lemon tart with praline ice cream

We went through a number of different lemon tart recipes before settling on this one, which I have to acknowledge is based on the brilliant River Cafe version. It uses a shocking amount of eggs, which made me very nervous at first, especially as we use expensive free-range eggs. But, probably the most important ingredient here is your own calm nature and patience, while you stand over the custard thickening on the stove top. That time spent whisking is where the tart gets its perfectly set texture from, a texture that holds about as much lemon flavour as is possible. No better way to finish a rich meal.

FOR THE PASTRY:

- 100g plain flour
- 50g cold unsalted butter
- 30g caster sugar
- 1 egg yolk

CUT THE BUTTER INTO SMALL DICE and rub into the flour, using the pulse facility of a food processor, or your fingers, until it resembles fine breadcrumbs. Transfer to a bowl and stir in the sugar. Lightly beat the egg yolk with a fork and add a little water, to give 25mls of liquid. Pour this into the flour and butter crumbs and mix it with a few judicious strokes of a wooden spoon until the pastry begins to come together. Now, knead the dough very briefly and lightly to get a smooth flattened ball. Wrap and refrigerate it for at least one hour. Take the pastry ball, roll it to fit a 10-inch flan tin and blind-bake it at 375°F (Gas Mark 5) for 10–15 minutes until lightly coloured.

FOR THE FILLING:

- 3 large lemons, rind and juice
- 175g caster sugar
- 3 eggs
- 5 egg yolks
- 150g unsalted butter, diced

BLIND BAKE THE PASTRY CASE at 375°F (Gas Mark 5), then turn the oven up to 450°F (Gas Mark 8).

Put all the ingredients except the butter into a saucepan over the lowest possible heat and start whisking, slowly but constantly, until the sugar has dissolved. Add in half the butter and continue whisking until the mixture starts to thicken. This will take about six to eight minutes, so be calm – faster whisking or a higher heat won't help the cause. Now add in the rest of the butter and carry on with the whisking until the custard is very thick – probably another five minutes or so. It is crucial that it does not come to the boil during this stage. Next pour it through a fine sieve into the bowl of a food mixer and use the electric whisk of the mixer to continue whisking until the filling is lukewarm. If you don't have a free-standing electric whisk, you'll just have to carry on by hand, but you'll probably want to give up and cry by now. Spare a thought for the dedicated folks who do this, day in, day out, for no more than the honour and glory. Pour the lemon filling into the prepared pastry case and bake it in a hot oven, 450°F (Gas Mark 8), for 12 minutes, maybe 13, but no more. It will be only slightly darker than when it went in, and may not appear to be set, but it will firm up as it cools. Leave it to cool completely, it is best eaten cold, with some praline ice cream, or just a blob of cream.

FOR THE PRALINE ICE CREAM:

- vanilla ice cream (see page 163)
- almond praline (see page 163)

WHILE MAKING THE RECIPE for vanilla ice cream, add a few spoonfuls of praline when the ice cream has firmed up to the consistency of whipped cream. Allow the praline to be folded in by the churning of the ice cream machine or, if you are doing this manually, stir it in gently. Just before the ice cream is fully frozen, test it to see if there is enough praline for your liking.

Chocolate-pecan brownie

If 'brownie' sounds like something innocuous you might have a couple of with your afternoon tea, try eating two of these. Rich and intensely chocolatey, they are as suitable for impressing at dinner as they are for a late-morning splurge. There is an awful lot of chocolate in the recipe and this makes the quality of the chocolate vital to the type of brownie you'll turn out. Chocolate with at least 55 per cent cocoa solids is needed, though the ideal here is 70 per cent. Half of the chocolate in the recipe is chopped into small pieces which will then melt into the cake as it bakes. We use small chocolate drops which are an ideal size for this, about the size of a fat pea, to give you a rough idea, but don't fret about it – any size will melt during a half hour's baking. We bake the brownies in a tin 12 inches by 8 and 1½ inches deep. A 10-inch square tin is similar. If you use a much smaller or bigger tin you will need to adjust the recipe.

- 450g dark chocolate
- 225g unsalted butter
- 225g caster sugar
- 3 eggs
- 2 tblspns strong coffee
- 75g plain flour
- 1 tsp baking powder
- pinch of salt
- 150g pecans, sliced
- 1 tsp vanilla essence

BUTTER A 10-INCH SQUARE TIN or similar and line the base of it with baking parchment or greaseproof paper. Take half the chocolate, roughly chop it and melt it with the butter over hot water. Allow this to cool a little. Chop the rest of the chocolate into small pieces. Beat together the sugar, eggs and coffee briefly, then add the melted chocolate and butter, and beat it again. Combine the remaining ingredients, including the chocolate pieces, and fold them into the sugar-egg mix. Pour this into the prepared tin and bake it at 375°F (Gas Mark 5) for 30–40 minutes.

Leave the cake to cool in the tin for at least an hour, then cut it into squares and turn it out. It is at its best eaten warm with vanilla ice cream, but is still good at room temperature. Stored in an airtight container, it will keep for a week.

Rhubarb shortbread

with butterscotch sauce

The challenge in a restaurant when dealing with the season's finest fruit is to present it at its simple best while making a dish interesting enough to take people's minds off the chocolate. Some fruits carry the extra burden of being loved and hated equally, and rhubarb is right up there with blackcurrants and gooseberries in that context. Given that only rhubarb lovers will order any dish with rhubarb, it is essential that it then has enough rhubarb to satisfy them, while still being pretty, interesting, etc etc. This recipe is one of those attempts to pull off that juggling feat. The serious rhubarb person will, however, be satisfied only by a large steaming bowl of stewed rhubarb or a mountain of rhubarb crumble. The rhubarb and biscuits can be done a day or more ahead, but make sure the rhubarb is at room temperature when you serve it.

FOR FOUR:

- 1 large bundle of rhubarb sticks
- 300g caster sugar
- 100g unsalted butter
- 150g plain flour
- rind of ½ orange

CHOP THE RHUBARB INTO PIECES of about 15mm long. Cook these very gently with 250g of sugar and one tablespoon of water until the rhubarb is just tender – it makes the world of difference if the rhubarb pieces don't totally disintegrate. Carefully transfer the rhubarb to a bowl to cool.

Preheat the oven to 375°F (Gas Mark 5). Cream the butter and 50g of sugar until fluffy, then beat in the flour and orange rind. Wrap this dough and chill it for 30 minutes, then roll it to about 5mm thickness and cut out round biscuits of about 8cm diameter. You will need three per person. Bake the biscuits on an oven tray covered with baking parchment for 20–25 minutes. They should be pale brown but not quite crisp – they will crisp fully as they cool.

- 100g light muscovado sugar
- 50g unsalted butter
- 500mls single or double cream
- icing sugar, to serve

TO MAKE THE BUTTERSCOTCH SAUCE, put the muscovado sugar, unsalted butter and 300mls of the cream into a pan, bring it slowly to a boil, then boil it for two minutes. Leave the sauce to cool to room temperature before using it. Whisk the remaining 200mls of cream until softly whipped.

Place a shortbread biscuit on each plate, spread a layer of cream on it, then pile on a generous tablespoon of rhubarb. Put another biscuit on that, then more cream and rhubarb, then a third biscuit. A light dusting of icing sugar finishes it off nicely. Pour a stream of the butterscotch sauce around the biscuits. Obviously a fork won't pass easily through that lot, so I tend to lean the third biscuit half-off the construction to make it easy for people who are nervous about demolishing pretty plates of food. But that's a restaurant thing and your guests won't be like that, will they?

Organic strawberries on a hazelnut pavlova

I must explain why I use the word 'organic' in this recipe. The strawberries we were getting were so delicious, so intensely flavoured, perfectly ripe and chaotically shaped that we had to serve them simply and in abundance. It would have been a crime to trick them out in a clever recipe, and I wanted to emphasize that it was the strawberries themselves that were the stars of the dish. If you do this dish with thinly flavoured, water-puffed strawberries, you will need to do a song and dance routine as well to get a smile from your guests. You could, of course serve the strawberries on a slice of an ordinary large pavlova, but these individual ones are no harder to make.

FOR EIGHT PAVLOVAS:

- 4 egg whites
- 240g caster sugar
- 40g hazelnuts, finely ground
- 1 tsp cornflour
- ½ tsp white wine vinegar
- 250mls single or double cream
- 800g organic strawberries
- a little icing sugar

PREHEAT AN OVEN to 250°F (Gas Mark ½). Whisk the egg whites until they are very stiff. Whisk in about a quarter of the sugar until the whites become glossy, then repeat this with three more batches of sugar. With the last batch of sugar, add the hazelnuts, cornflour and vinegar. Line an oven tray or trays with baking parchment. Spoon the meringue on to the parchment in roughly circular mounds of about 6cm diameter but quite tall, say about 5cm. Make as many as you have meringue and room for, they won't go to waste. Level the tops and put them in the oven for 75 minutes. Then turn off the oven but leave the pavlovas in there for a further hour. Check them occasionally during this time, however, as you don't want to end up with chalky, dry meringues instead. To be proper pavlova only the outsides can be crisp, the inside must still have that soft, melt-in-the-mouth texture of beaten egg white. When you are confident that your pavlovas have found this perfect balance, take them from the oven and leave them to cool.

Whip the cream until it is stiff enough to stand up on its own. Take about 100g of the strawberries, puree them, sieve them and add a little icing sugar to this sauce. Make sure the rest of the strawberries are at room temperature, take their little green hats off and chop any over-sized monsters in half. If you doubt their sweetness, sprinkle a little sugar over them up to half an hour before you serve them.

Place a pavlova in the centre of each plate with a 1–2cm layer of whipped cream on top, then place as many strawberries on top and around the pavlova as is physically possible and edible. Pour a stream of the strawberry sauce around and over each pavlova too.

Iced tiramisu terrine with coffee syrup

I wasn't too comfortable with the dessert squad using 'tiramisu' in the title of this dish, even though in savoury dishes I often use familiar words and names of dishes as signposts to the general territory of a new dish. There's something about that word, though, and one night a woman sent her terrine back, saying 'that's not a tiramisu, I make great tiramisu and that one doesn't even ...'. So let me say now that this is a layered frozen dessert that has some of the flavours of a traditional Italian dish. Oh, and it's divine, especially with the extra coffee kick of the syrup. Make sure the sponge has enough alcohol in it to prevent it freezing too hard. This recipe makes enough to fill one 2lb loaf tin, which will comfortably satisfy eight non-pedants.

FOR SIX TO EIGHT:

- 4 eggs
- 115g caster sugar
- 115g plain flour
- 1 tsp baking powder

- 150mls marsala
- 250mls single or double cream
- 3 egg yolks
- 150g caster sugar
- 250mls water

- 1 tblspn icing sugar
- 2 tblspns very strong coffee
- 1 tblspn Tia Maria coffee liqueur
- 250g mascarpone

PREHEAT AN OVEN to 375°F (Gas Mark 5). Butter a 16cm square cake tin or similar and line the base with baking parchment.

Whisk the eggs and the 115g of sugar until thick and creamy, then fold in the flour and baking powder. Bake the sponge in the prepared tin for 40–50 minutes, until just firm to the touch. When the sponge is cooled, take it from the tin, slice it in half horizontally and sprinkle three tablespoons of the marsala over the pieces.

Whisk the cream until softly whipped and set it aside. Then whisk the egg yolks until pale and creamy. Bring the 150g of sugar and 250mls of water to a boil in a pan and boil for a minute to dissolve the sugar. Pour this on to the yolks, whisking all the time until they become frothy, then gently whisk in the whipped cream and the rest of the marsala. Freeze this custard, preferably using an ice cream machine.

Stir the icing sugar, coffee and Tia Maria into the mascarpone. Line a 2lb loaf tin with a double layer of overhanging clingfilm. Spread in one third of the 'ice cream', cover it with a layer of sponge followed by half of the mascarpone. Repeat these layers, then put in the final third of the ice cream. Fold over the overhanging clingfilm, then freeze the terrine. Turn it out on to a plate before slicing it. If the terrine seems to have frozen very hard, move it to a fridge for half an hour before you serve it.

FOR THE COFFEE SYRUP:

- 300mls strong coffee
- 150g sugar
- 1 tblspn coffee beans

BRING THE COFFEE and sugar to the boil and simmer them until reduced to half the original volume. Toss in the beans and leave the syrup to cool. Spoon some syrup over and around each slice of terrine.

Little summer puddings
with poached nectarines

I was thinking of converting this recipe to one large pudding in the traditional style, but the construction of these takes only a few minutes more – honestly, I timed it. We use a simple sponge for the casing and you will need six small individual pudding bowls or good-sized cups or ramekins – anything that will make a decent-sized pudding for one in an attractive shape. As well as the poached nectarines, we often serve the vanilla custard on page 158 with these puddings, though a little lightly whipped cream is almost as good.

FOR SIX:

- 4 eggs
- 115g caster sugar
- 115g plain flour
- 1 tsp baking powder
- 600g summer berries – two or three of raspberries, blueberries, redcurrants, strawberries, blackcurrants
- 300g caster sugar

PREHEAT AN OVEN to 375°F (Gas Mark 5). Butter a 16cm square cake tin or similar and line the base with baking parchment.

Whisk the eggs and the 115g of sugar until thick and creamy, then fold in the flour and baking powder. Bake the sponge in the prepared tin for 40–50 minutes, until just firm to the touch.

Put the berries and 300g of sugar in a pan and heat them very slowly until the sugar dissolves and the berries almost come to a boil, then leave to cool. Strain off the syrup and pass it through a fine sieve to remove any pips.

Cut circles from the sponge to line the bases of your chosen pudding moulds and larger ones to fit the tops, then cut slices to line the insides of the moulds. The sponge pieces should be about 5mm thick. Dip them in the berry syrup and line the moulds as neatly as you can. Fill the puddings with the fruit and gently press the larger sponge circles on top. Chill the puddings for a few hours, preferably overnight.

- 4 ripe nectarines
- 100g sugar
- 150mls water

PUT THE NECTARINES in a bowl or pan, pour boiling water over them and leave them for one minute. The skins should peel away easily now. Slice the nectarines into wedges, six or eight from each one. Dissolve the sugar in the 150mls water and bring to the boil. Add in the nectarine slices and simmer them gently for six to eight minutes, checking them often to avoid overcooking them. Serve the nectarines at room temperature with the chilled puddings.

Blackcurrant fool

with little cinnamon biscuits

Fool is such a strange dessert, strangely named. Many people would make their excuses rather than eat a bowl of lightly whipped cream flavoured with one of the sourer fruits. For others, it is heaven and I love to watch their faces as the first spoonful slips down. Certainly it works best with that group of fruits which divide people: rhubarb, gooseberries, blackcurrants; although Mags makes an incredible fool of apricots, the recipe for which, she says, we will have to wait. Of course you could go out and buy some delicate confectionery instead of the cute little biscuits below, but they are easy to make and you'll feel so pleased with yourself.

FOR FOUR TO SIX:

- 300g caster sugar
- 300mls water
- 500g blackcurrants
- 300mls single or double cream

THE BISCUITS:

- 50g butter
- 25g caster sugar
- 75g plain flour
- ½ tsp ground cinnamon

PUT THE SUGAR and water in a pan and bring it slowly to the boil, then add in the blackcurrants and simmer them on very low heat for five or six minutes, until the currants are soft. Puree the currants and their cooking liquid and pass the puree through a fine sieve to take out seeds and skins, then leave it to cool. Whisk the cream until softly whipped. When the currant puree is cold, fold in about two thirds of the cream, taste it and fold in more cream as you see fit – you may not need all of it.

Preheat the oven to 375°F (Gas Mark 5). Beat together the butter and sugar until fluffy, then briefly beat in the flour and cinnamon. Use your hands to bring the dough together, wrap it and chill it for an hour to firm up. This may take longer, depending on your fridge, but don't try to roll the dough until it is firm. On a lightly floured surface, roll the dough quite thin, then cut small biscuit shapes from it – you know, hearts, stars, diamonds, Christmas trees, alphabets or good old useful circles. Bake the biscuits on parchment-lined oven trays until lightly coloured, about 20 minutes. Leave them to cool fully on the trays before using or storing them.

Serve the fool in bowls or tall glasses with a multitude of tiny biscuits on the side.

Dark and white chocolate mousses

on a coffee sauce

Also known as the odd couple, this pair of mousses are opposites in many ways, though almost identical in their content. One is dark, heavy, intense; the other white, airily light and delicate. The only thing holding together the texture of the mousse is whipped cream, no gelatines nor other support systems, and almost the only flavour is chocolate, as much as the cream can possibly hold up. It hardly needs to be said that the best chocolate you can get your hands on is vital in these circumstances. We use a dark chocolate with 70 per cent cocoa solids, though anything from 55 per cent up is fine. White chocolate, often sneered at by chocolate snobs, is harder to judge. I think the best guide is to look for a simple and short list of ingredients headed by sugar, cocoa butter and milk powder. Nasty tasting artificial sweeteners should sound the loudest alarm bells. The quantities for each mousse, dark and white, will separately feed six people, as will the coffee sauce. If you want to halve the recipes to make six portions of one scoop of each mousse, you will have to whisk the single egg and egg yolk together and divide them up when stirring them into the chocolates. Otherwise the recipe halves very easily.

DARK MOUSSE FOR SIX:

- 150g dark chocolate, chopped
- 1 egg
- 1 egg yolk
- 325mls single or double cream
- 2 tsps brandy

WHITE MOUSSE FOR SIX:

- 150g white chocolate, chopped
- 1 egg
- 1 egg yolk
- 350mls single or double cream
- 2 tsps kirsch

THE TECHNIQUE FOR BOTH MOUSSES IS IDENTICAL, except that the melted dark chocolate needs to cool only a little before the next step, whereas the white chocolate won't blend smoothly with the egg unless it is cooled almost to room temperature. If you want to do both mousses at the same time you will need six clean, dry bowls, and you should melt the white chocolate first but finish the dark mousse first.

Put the chocolate in a bowl over hot water and allow it to melt slowly. Set it aside to cool a little. In another bowl, over the hot water, whisk the egg and egg yolk until they become thick and creamy. Next, whisk the cream until it is softly but firmly whipped, then briefly whisk in the brandy (or kirsch). When it has cooled a little, stir the chocolate and egg together. Then fold this into the whipped cream.

Put the mousses in a covered container in a fridge to chill and firm up; they can then be served in scoops using an ice cream scoop or a spoon. Alternatively, one or both mousses could be put directly into glasses or bowls and allowed to chill in those. The mousses, once they have firmed up, should hold their texture for at least a day, and maybe two.

COFFEE SAUCE FOR SIX:

- 3 egg yolks
- 50mls strong black coffee
- 30g icing sugar
- 50mls single or double cream
- 1 tblspn brandy or Tia Maria

IN YET ANOTHER BOWL over hot water, slowly whisk the egg yolks, coffee and sugar together until quite thick. Off the heat, stir in the cream and the brandy or Tia Maria, which will thin the sauce again to a silky pouring consistency.

Orange and cardamom bombette
with pistachio wafers

Curry and popadams for dessert, as Mr Foley, book designer, gourmet and wit, calls it. The preparation seems like a lot of work, but can all be done over the days before you need the bombettes and, of course, an ice cream maker is a huge help, especially for the sorbet. The lovely photo of this dessert features a bombette which is actually pure sorbet, one of a sneaky shortcut batch made by someone I foolishly left into my kitchen briefly. It looks just like the real thing and wasn't discovered until both the photographer and the lazy boy had departed.

FOR SIX BOMBETTES:

- 2 tblspns whole cardamom seeds
- 200mls single or double cream
- 200mls milk
- 3 egg yolks
- 100g caster sugar
- rind and juice of 2 oranges

FOR 0.5 LITRE ORANGE SORBET:

- 250g caster sugar
- 220mls water
- rind and juice of 3 oranges
- 1 egg white

FOR 12 WAFERS:

- 50g shelled pistachio nuts
- 10g plain flour
- 45g caster sugar
- 40g egg white
- 15g unsalted butter, melted and slightly warm

REMOVE the cardamom seeds from their shells. Put them in a pan with the cream and milk, warm it gently, though not to boiling point. Take the pan from the heat and leave it for 15 minutes, then pass it through a fine sieve to remove all but the finest cardamom powder.

Whisk the egg yolks and sugar until thick and creamy. At the same time, reheat the infused milk and cream. With the whisk now on low speed, slowly pour in the liquid, then return this custard to the pan and, over a low heat, stir until it has thickened enough to coat the back of a spoon.

Boil the orange juice and rind in a small pan to reduce the liquid by half – then add it to the custard. Leave it to cool completely before freezing it in an ice cream maker.

To make the sorbet, put the caster sugar, water and orange rind in a small pan, bring it to a boil and simmer for two minutes. Leave it to cool before stirring in the orange juice and egg white. Freeze the sorbet in an ice cream machine.

To finish the bombettes, fill six moulds of about 150mls each with some of the orange-cardamom ice cream, scooping out a hollow in the centre. Fill this hollow with some sorbet, leaving enough room for a covering layer of the ice cream. Put the bombettes in the freezer to firm up again. To remove the bombettes from their moulds, run each one under hot water for a few seconds, then turn the bombettes out on to plates. A gentle but firm tap will encourage any stubborn ones.

To make the pistachio wafers, first grind the pistachios as finely as possible, then pass the grounds through a fine sieve. Re-grind the nuts that didn't pass through until all 50g has been successfully sieved. This may seem tedious but large pieces will destroy the texture of your wafers. Now combine the pistachio, flour and sugar and stir in first the egg white and then the butter.

Preheat the oven to 350°F (Gas Mark 4). On a tray lined with baking parchment, use a teaspoon to form very thin circles of the wafer mix with diameters of 8–10cm. If the circles are so thin they're see-through in places, you've got the right consistency. Bake the wafers in the oven for eight to ten minutes, until they are lightly toasted. As soon as they are taken from the oven, drape each one over a rolling pin, wooden spoon, broom handle or suchlike for a few seconds to allow it to cool into a curved shape. The wafers will store well for a few days in very dry, sealed conditions, though they are so fragile you will lose a few every time you move the container.

Gooseberry-almond tartlets

with an amaretto custard

This dish was put on the Café menu because Kim'n'Ian of Hollyhill farm asked if we had any use for gooseberries, then wound up our curiosity by mentioning that they had three different types, ranging in sweetness and colour shading. Then Mags, Paradiso baker and pastry cook, came up with this lovely way to dress them up for dinner without losing any of their unique gooseberryness. You know how some people hate gooseberries? Well, they'll hate this. The pastry is a strange affair, having no flour and needing no shaping, as you'll see from the instructions. But it turns out thin, crisp and very sweet which is perfect for gooseberries.

FOR EIGHT:

- 80g unsalted butter
- 80g ground almonds
- 80g caster sugar
- 600g gooseberries
- 400g caster sugar
- 100g apricot jam
- 1 tsp lemon juice
- 1 tblspn water

PREHEAT THE OVEN to 350°F (Gas Mark 4). Cream the butter, almonds and 80g of sugar. Lightly butter eight shallow tartlet tins. Put one rounded dessertspoon of the pastry in each, and flatten it slightly with the back of the spoon, but don't attempt to shape it into the tin in any serious way. The pastry will rise a little in the baking and collapse to form a shallow-lipped base. Anyway, bake the pastries for 20–25 minutes, until lightly browned, then leave them to cool in the trays.

Meanwhile, place the gooseberries and the 400g of sugar in a heavy pan and cook them very gently over a very low heat, until the berries have softened but still hold their shape. Tip the berries and their syrup into a bowl and leave them to cool to room temperature. The apricot glaze needs to be warm and thickly pourable, so make it now and warm it up when you need it, or do it just before serving. Simply heat the jam, lemon juice and water together in a pan until pourable, then sieve the result.

To serve the tartlets, remove the pastries from their tins (very carefully – they're quite fragile), place them on plates, spoon a generous pile of gooseberries into each, and brush a thin layer of glaze over each pile. Pour a small pool of custard on to the plates, and put the jug on the table for the custard-freaks to indulge their cravings.

FOR THE CUSTARD:

- 3 egg yolks
- 60g caster sugar
- 300mls single or double cream
- 1 tblspn Amaretto liqueur

WHISK THE YOLKS AND SUGAR together until fluffy. In a pan, heat the cream gently, but don't boil it! Pour the cream over the egg and sugar, stir it in gently and return the lot to the pan. Now, heat the custard very gently, stirring all the time, until it has thickened to a good pouring consistency then stir in the Amaretto – fans of extra-thick custard will risk scrambling the eggs if they go on too long in search of their grail. The custard is at its best if left to cool a little to just warm, but can also be used hot, cold or even carefully reheated.

Ginger-sautéed pears

with iced mascarpone

Pears, the definitive winter fruit, gently cooked with ginger and butter make a perfect winter dessert. We use a shop-bought jar of ginger pieces in syrup, sold as 'ginger nuts'. They are very sweet, a little spicy and somehow nostalgic. The iced mascarpone, light and creamy in its raw state, is rich and dense and melts into the gingery syrup at its own pace.

FOR FOUR:

- 2 egg yolks
- 80g icing sugar
- 225g mascarpone
- 2 drops vanilla essence
- 6 ripe but firm pears
- 4 walnut-sized lumps of ginger in syrup
- 80g butter
- 60mls white wine
- juice of ½ lemon

BEAT THE EGG YOLKS with the sugar until creamy, then beat in the mascarpone and vanilla. To freeze this you will get a slightly softer texture using an ice cream machine, though it will always be dense so the difference isn't as much as usual.

Slice the pears into six segments and take out the cores and seeds. Slice the ginger thinly. Melt the butter in a heavy, wide frying pan and cook the pears and ginger over a low to moderate heat, turning them occasionally, until the pears have softened a little and begun to brown at the edges. This will take between five and ten minutes, depending on the pears. Now pour in the wine, lemon juice and three tablespoons of the ginger syrup. Allow it to boil for only a few seconds before sharing out the pear slices and their sauce. Serve a scoop of the iced mascarpone with each portion.

White chocolate torte

with dark chocolate sorbet

This is a very rich cake which will easily serve twelve or more as a dessert, maybe fewer as a mid-afternoon snack.

- 200g white chocolate, chopped
- 200g unsalted butter
- 4 eggs, separated
- 200g caster sugar
- 125g plain flour
- 50g ground almonds
- 2 tblspns Amaretto liqueur

- 2 tblspns caster sugar
- 150g white chocolate, chopped
- 25g dark chocolate, chopped (optional)

PREHEAT THE OVEN to 350°F (Gas Mark 4). Butter a 23cm cake tin and line the base with baking parchment.

In a bowl over hot water, melt the 200g of white chocolate and butter together. Whisk the egg whites until stiff, set them aside. Whisk the egg yolks and the sugar together until fluffy, then beat in the melted chocolate and butter. Combine the flour and almonds and fold them into the mix, then fold in the egg whites. Put this cake mix in the prepared tin and bake it for 60–80 minutes. Leave it to cool in the tin, then turn it out on to a wire rack. Prick holes all over the torte and drizzle the Amaretto over it.

Make a sugar syrup by putting the two tablespoons of sugar in a small pan with twice that volume of water, bringing it to a boil slowly, then allowing it to cool. You probably won't need that much but it would be hard to make less. Melt the 150g of white chocolate gently, then stir in some sugar syrup until the chocolate becomes spreadable. Pour it over the torte and use a spatula or pallet knife to spread it evenly over the torte, including the sides. Now melt the dark chocolate and use it to draw a decorative pattern on the white torte.

DARK CHOCOLATE SORBET:

- 200mls water
- 50mls milk
- 75g sugar
- 20g cocoa powder
- 50g dark chocolate, chopped
- 1 egg white

PUT EVERYTHING EXCEPT THE CHOPPED CHOCOLATE and the egg white in a small pan and bring it to the boil, whisking constantly, then simmer it for two minutes. Take the pan off the heat and whisk in the chocolate until it has melted. Leave this to cool completely. Add one lightly whisked egg white and freeze the sorbet in an ice cream machine. If you don't have one, put the sorbet mix in the freezer, whisk it occasional until nearly frozen, then fold in the whisked egg white and put it back in the freezer until fully frozen.

Baked praline-stuffed peaches

with rosewater syrup and vanilla ice cream

This is a very difficult dish to maintain on a restaurant menu because peaches need to be close to perfectly ripe to justify their exotic, luscious reputation; and a steady supply of ripe peaches is frustratingly hard to maintain. If you find a batch, chances are you'll eat a couple on the way home, so buy extra. The only quantity in this recipe that caters accurately for six people is the number of peaches. Fret not, the ice cream, praline and syrup recipes work perfectly, but they are convenient and sensible minimal volumes to set about making. Praline keeps for ages in a well-sealed container so you might even want to make double this amount; and I've never yet seen ice cream go to waste. Some people like their praline to be a fine ground while others like a certain challenge to their dentalwork in their pleasure. If you are this way inclined, warn your guests first.

FOR THE PRALINE:

- 100g caster sugar
- 60g whole almonds, lightly roasted

FOR THE ROSEWATER SYRUP:

- 100g caster sugar
- 100g clear honey
- 100mls water
- 2 tsps rosewater

- 6 large ripe peaches
- 1 egg yolk
- 50g butter, melted

FIRST MAKE THE PRALINE. Put the sugar in a small, heavy-bottomed pan over the lowest possible heat. Leave it until it has melted and turned golden brown. Immediately you are satisfied, stir in the nuts quickly and remove the lot to a parchment-lined plate or tray and leave it to cool. The sugar should become glass-hard. Break up the praline into smallish pieces, then use a food processor to chop to the texture you want. Store the praline in a dry, well-sealed container.

To make the syrup, simply put the ingredients in a small pan, bring it to the boil and boil for three minutes, then leave it to cool. You should get an almost-clear, slightly thickened pouring consistency. If it is too thick, add a little more water and bring it back to the boil for a few seconds, then cool it again.

Preheat the oven to 375°F (Gas Mark 5). Put the peaches in a bowl and pour over enough boiling water to cover. In two minutes, the skins should slip off easily. Halve them and remove the stones. Take enough praline to fill the twelve cavities and stir in the egg yolk. Fill the peach halves and place them in a shallow, lightly buttered, oven dish, filled side down. Brush the tops with a little butter and bake for 20–30 minutes until they are tender and lightly coloured.

Serve two peach halves per person with a tablespoon of syrup poured over and around each portion, and a scoop of vanilla ice cream.

FOR THE VANILLA ICE CREAM (makes 1 litre):

- 5 egg yolks
- 125g caster sugar
- 0.5 litres milk
- 1 tsp vanilla extract
- 125mls single or double cream

WHISK THE EGG YOLKS and sugar together until they become thick and pale. In a pan, heat the milk almost to boiling, then pour it in a slow, steady stream on to the eggs and sugar, with the whisk running on low speed. Return this custard to the pan, heat it gently and simmer, stirring all the time, until it is thick enough to coat the back of a spoon. Strain it through a fine sieve, stir in the vanilla and leave it to cool. When it is cold, add the cream and freeze it, preferably using an ice cream maker.

Index

aioli
basil, 68
from herb oils, 40
almond
carrot and feta terrine, 74
filling, with chilli and scallion, for couscous-crusted aubergine, 126–7
and gooseberry tartlets, 158
Moroccan-spiced vegetable and almond pastries, 122–3
praline ice cream, 142
pumpkin and spring cabbage dolma, 124
amaretto custard, 158
Ardsallagh cheese, 12
with broad bean, spinach and beetroot salad, 50
artichokes
pan-fried, parmesan-stuffed fritters, 68
salad Tobias, 46
asparagus
chard and goats' brie crêpe, 103
and Gabriel cheese gratin, 78
mangetout and pinenut risotto, 113–14
aubergines
broad beans, red onions and chillies with pasta in basil oil, 121
and cabbage in coconut-cumin pancakes, 109
-chilli rolls, 135–7
couscous-crusted, 126–7
gamelastra, 133–4
grilled, 19
ratatouille, 90
sticky rice rolls, 71
tomato and mozzarella tart, 111
avocado
salsa, 33
watercress and new potato salad, 52

balsamic vinegar
dressing, 48
-roasted beetroot, 21
vinaigrette, 64
basil
aioli, 68
oil, 39
pesto, 37
batter
deep-fried courgette flower parcels of sheep's cheese and pinenuts, 62
tempura, 57
beetroot
balsamic-roasted, 21
broad bean and spinach salad, 50
chilled soup, 58–9
mousse, 66
roasted, 21
sweet-spiced cream, 70–1
biscuits
cinnamon, 152
pistachio wafers, 156
shortbread, 146
blackcurrants
fool, 152
little summer puddings, 150
breads, 16–18
focaccia sandwich, 18
grilled ciabatta with olive and goats' cheese, 90
grilled ciabatta with roasted vegetable ratatouille, 90
olive-grilled ciabatta, 76
onion, with rosemary and tomato, 16–17
tomato crostini, 48
brie, roasted pepper and olive tartlets, 64
broad bean
aubergines, red onions and chillies with pasta in basil oil, 121
spinach and beetroot salad, 50
broccoli, purple sprouting, with new potatoes, 61
brownies, chocolate-pecan, 144
buckwheat noodles with mushroom stir fry, 98
butterbean, squash and leek stew, 92–4
butterscotch sauce, 146

cabbage
and aubergines in coconut-cumin pancakes, 109
sesame-fried, 29
spring, pumpkin and almond dolma, 124
capers and pinenut stuffing in roasted sweet pepper rolls, 106
cardamom
-lime pancakes, 131–2
and orange bombette, 156
carrot
almond and feta terrine, 74
Moroccan-spiced vegetable and almond pastries, 122–3
roasted, 117
cashews
Thai tofu-cashew fritters, 128–9
celeriac
potato and hazelnut soup, 60
and salsify fritters, deep-fried, 83
chard, asparagus and goats' brie crêpe, 103
cheese, 11–12
Ardsallagh goats' cheese with broad bean, spinach and beetroot salad, 50
asparagus, chard and goats' brie crêpe, 103
asparagus and Gabriel cheese gratin, 78
aubergines, tomato and mozzarella tart, 111
baked leek, walnut and Gubbeen crêpe, 101
blue cheese cream, 83
braised spinach parcels of feta, green pepper and caramelized onion, 70–1
carrot, almond and feta terrine, 74
corn pancakes of roasted pepper, red onion and goats' cheese, 72
courgette flower parcels of sheep's cheese and pinenuts, 62
feta cheese with pumpkin, almond and spring cabbage, 124
focaccia sandwich, 18
fresh mozzarella and tomato salad, 54
Gabriel cheese gougeres, 94
goats' cheese and olive ciabatta, 90
goats' cheese, pinenut and oven-roasted tomato charlotte, 104
grilled polenta with parmesan, 45
leek and parmesan sauce, 138–9
leek and smoked cheese mash, 24
oyster mushroom and smoked Gubbeen ravioli, 69
pan-fried, parmesan-stuffed artichoke fritters, 68
peperonata with olive-grilled ciabatta and parmesan, 76
potato and blue cheese cakes, 102
with purple sprouting broccoli and new potatoes, 61
roasted pepper, olive and brie tartlets, 64
spinach, leek and stilton tart, 111
summer vegetables with mixed leaves and Knockalara sheep's cheese, 47
tomato salad with rocket pesto and Knockalara sheep's cheese, 54
chermoula, 35
chickpeas
with chillies, 28
felafel, 31
with spinach, lemon and cumin, 126–7
chilli, 10
almond and scallion filling for couscous-crusted aubergine, 126–7
and aubergine rolls, 135–7
aubergines, broad beans and red onions with pasta in basil oil, 121
chickpeas with, 28
and chilli sauce, sweet, 98
-coconut cream, 86
-coriander pesto, 38
-fennel salsa, 33
filling, with almond and scallion, for couscous-crusted aubergine, 126–7
pistachio, green chilli and yoghurt kofta, 131–2
-roasted squash, 27
-rosemary oil, 39
squash, butterbean and leek stew, 92–4
and ginger sauce, sweet, 98
chive
and roasted garlic cream, 106–7
chocolate
dark chocolate sorbet, 162
dark and white chocolate mousses, 154
-pecan brownies, 144
white chocolate torte, 162
ciabatta
grilled with goats' cheese and olive, with roasted vegetable ratatouille, 90
olive-grilled, with peperonata, 76
cider
flageolet beans in rosemary and, 102–3
and thyme, mushrooms in, 97
cinnamon biscuits, 152
coconut
and chilli cream, 86
and cumin pancakes, 109
sauce with lime and coriander, 100
-stewed vegetables, 128–9
-tomato sauce, 131–2
coffee
sauce, 154
syrup with iced tiramisu terrine, 149
coriander
-chilli pesto, 38
coconut sauce with lime and, 100
and cucumber yoghurt sauce, 122–3
-green pepper salsa, 32
-lime oil, 40
tomato and puy lentil concasse, 82
corn pancakes of roasted pepper, red onion and goats' cheese, 72
courgette flower parcels of sheep's cheese and pinenuts, 62
couscous
-crusted aubergine, 126–7
lemon-buttered, 30
roasted roots and couscous pilaff, 117
crêpes *see* pancakes
crostini, tomato, 48
cucumber
and coriander yoghurt sauce, 122–3
and green bean salad, Thai, 51
soured cream and scallion garnish, 59

cumin
and coconut pancakes, 109
and lemon cream, 135–7
with spinach, chickpeas and lemon, 126–7
desserts, 141–63
dressings
balsamic, 48
balsamic vinaigrette, 64
blue cheese cream, 83
pesto, 47
roasted peanut-citrus, 51
Spanish paprika and yoghurt, 52
tapenade, 50

egg dishes, 10
amaretto custard, 158
aubergine, tomato and mozzarella tart, 111
feta custard with pumpkin, almond and spring cabbage, 124
hazelnut pavlova, 148
herbed potato tortilla, 91
mushroom, pak choy and eggroll stir fry, 98
savoury tarts, 111
spinach, leek and stilton tart, 111

felafel, 31
fennel
braised, 24
-chilli salsa, 33
and orange scented yoghurt, 66
and penne, green peppers and olives, 118
feta
braised spinach parcels of green pepper and caramelized onion, 70–1
carrot and almond terrine, 74
custard with pumpkin, almond and spring cabbage, 124
flageolet beans in cider and rosemary, 102–3
focaccia sandwich, 18
fool, blackcurrant, 152
fritters
pan-fried parmesan-stuffed artichoke, 68
deep-fried salsify and celeriac, 83
parsnip, and wild rice, 96–7
potato and blue cheese cakes, 102
Thai tofu-cashew, 128–9

Gabriel cheese, 11, 12
and asparagus gratin, 78
gougeres, 94
garlic
green beans with lemon and, 20
roasted, and chive cream, 106–7
roasted, and parsley oil, 118
ginger
broth with three wontons, 80–1
and chilli sauce, sweet, 98
gingered kale, walnut and pumpkin gratin, 135–7
gingered pumpkin cream, 116
gingered sweet potato spring rolls, 86
oyster mushrooms in gingered butter, 84
-roasted sweet potatoes, 26
-sautéed pears, 160
-shoyu dip, 57
gooseberry-almond tarlets, 158
gougeres, 94
green beans
and cucumber salad, Thai, 51
with garlic and lemon, 20
green peppers
braised spinach parcels of feta and caramelized onion, 70–1
and coriander salsa, 32
with penne, fennel and olives, 118
greens
noodles, tofu and leeks, 100
wilted, 20
see also kale
Gubbeen, 12
baked leek and walnut crêpe, 101
smoked, and leek mash, 24
smoked, and oyster mushroom ravioli, 69

harissa-sweet pepper oil, 34
hazelnut
celeriac and potato soup, 60
pavlova with organic strawberries, 148
roasted pumpkin with lemon-hazelnut risotto stuffing, 138–9
herbed potato tortilla, 91

ice cream
orange and cardamom bombette, 156
praline, 142
vanilla, 163
iced mascarpone, 160
iced tiramisu terrine with coffee syrup, 149

kale
gingered, and walnut and pumpkin gratin, 135–7
with pistachio, green chilli and yoghurt kofta, 131–2
puy lentil and tomato concasse, 101
Knockalara sheep's cheese, 11, 12
with deep-fried courgette flower parcels and pinenuts, 62
with summer vegetables and mixed leaves, 47
with tomato salad and rocket pesto, 54

leeks
baked walnut and Gubbeen crêpe, 101
noodles, tofu and greens, 100
and parmesan sauce, 138–9
and pinenut timbale, 82
sautéed, 60
and smoked cheese mash, 24
spinach and stilton tart, 111
spinach and tomatoes with pasta ribbons in lemon sauce, 120
squash and butterbean stew, 92–4
lemon
-buttered couscous, 30
-cumin cream, 135–7
green beans with garlic and, 20
-hazelnut risotto stuffing with roasted pumpkin, 138–9
sauce, and pasta ribbons, 120
with spinach, chickpeas and cumin, 126–7
tart with praline ice cream, 142
lentils *see* puy lentils
lime
-cardamom pancakes, 131–2
coconut sauce with coriander and, 100
-coriander oil, 40

main dishes, 89–139
maize *see* polenta
mangetout *see* peas
mascarpone, iced, 160
Moroccan dishes
spiced vegetable and almond pastries, 122–3
mousse
beetroot, 66
dark and white chocolate, 154
mozzarella
aubergine, tomato and mozzarella tart, 111
and tomato salad, 54
mushrooms
in cider and thyme, 97
oyster, pan-fried, 115
oyster, pan-fried in gingered butter, 84
oyster, and smoked Gubbeen ravioli, 69
pak choy and eggroll stir fry, 98

nectarines, poached, 150
nuts *see* almonds; cashews; hazelnuts; peanuts; pecans; pistachio; walnuts

oils, 10–11
olive oil
aioli from herb oils, 40
basil aioli, 68
harissa-sweet pepper oil, 34
infused, 39–40
peperonata with olive-grilled ciabatta, 76
roasted garlic-parsley oil, 118
olives
black olive tapenade, 35
and grilled ciabatta, 76
penne with fennel and green peppers, 118
roasted pepper and brie tartlets, 64
onions
bread with rosemary and tomato, 16–17
caramelized, braised spinach parcels of feta, green pepper and, 70–1
red, and aubergines, broad beans and chillies with pasta in basil oil, 121
red, in corn pancakes of roasted pepper and goats' cheese, 72
watercress and red onion risotto, 115
orange
and cardamom bombette, 156
and fennel scented yoghurt, 66
organic strawberries on a hazelnut pavlova, 148
oyster mushrooms
pan-fried, 115
pan-fried in gingered butter, 84
and smoked Gubbeen ravioli, 69

pak choy
mushroom and eggroll stir fry, 98
pancakes
asparagus, chard and goats' brie crêpe, 103
baked leek, walnut and Gubbeen crêpe, 101
cardamom-lime, 131–2
coconut-cumin, 109
corn, of roasted pepper, red onion and goats' cheese, 72
paprika
and sage butter, 69
and yoghurt dressing, 52
parmesan
and grilled polenta, 45
and leek sauce, 138–9
pan-fried stuffed artichoke fritters, 68
with peperonata and olive-grilled ciabatta, 76
with purple sprouting broccoli and new potatoes, 61
with rocket and flat-leaf parsley salad, 48
parsley
flat-leaf, and rocket salad, 48
and roasted garlic oil, 118
parsnip
fritters and wild rice, 96–7
Moroccan-spiced vegetable and almond pastries, 122–3
roasted, 117, 138–9
pasta, 118–21
in basil oil, 121
buckwheat noodles with mushroom, pak choy and eggroll stir fry, 98
noodles, tofu, leeks and greens, 100
oyster mushroom and smoked Gubbeen ravioli, 69
penne with fennel, green peppers and olives, 118
ribbons in lemon sauce, 120
pastry, 110
almond (no flour), 158
filo, 122
pavlova, hazelnut, 148
peaches
baked praline-stuffed, 163
poached nectarines, 150
peanuts
roasted peanut-citrus dressing, 51
pears, ginger-sautéed, 160
peas
asparagus, mangetout and pinenut risotto, 113–14
pecans
chocolate-pecan brownies, 144
peperonata, 76
peppers
corn pancakes of roasted pepper, red onion and goats' cheese, 72
harissa-sweet pepper oil, 34

peperonata with olive-grilled ciabatta, 76
roasted, 19
roasted, olive and brie tartlets, 64
roasted sweet pepper rolls of caper-pinenut stuffing, 106
sauce of roasted, 133–4
sweet, concasse, 126–7
see also green peppers; red peppers; yellow peppers

pesto, 37–8
basil, 37
coriander-chilli, 38
rocket, 37
sundried tomato, 38

pineapple chutney, 34

pinenuts
asparagus and mangetout risotto, 113–14
and caper stuffing in roasted sweet pepper rolls, 106
courgette flower parcels of sheep's cheese and, 62
goats' cheese and oven-roasted tomato charlotte, 104
and leek timbale, 82
see also pesto

pistachio
green chilli and yoghurt kofta, 131–2
wafers, 156

polenta, 41
croutons, 133–4
grilled, 45

potatoes
and blue cheese cakes, 102
celeriac and hazelnut soup, 60
herbed tortilla, 91
leek and smoked cheese mash, 24
new, and purple spouting broccoli, 61
new, watercress and avocado salad, 52
spiced roast, 26
wasabi mash, 23
see also sweet potatoes

praline
ice cream, 142
-stuffed peaches, baked, 163

pumpkin
almond and spring cabbage dolma, 124
gingered kale and walnut gratin, 135–7
gingered pumpkin cream, 116
roasted, and lemon-hazelnut risotto stuffing, 138–9
roasted, and radicchio risotto, 116
see also squash

purple sprouting broccoli with new potatoes, 61

puy lentils
in basil oil, 104
braised, 25
tomato and coriander concasse, 82
tomato and kale concasse, 101

radicchio and roasted pumpkin risotto, 116

ratatouille, roasted vegetable, 90

red peppers
corn pancakes of red onion, goats' cheese and roasted, 72
harissa-sweet pepper oil, 34

rhubarb shortbread, 146

rice
asparagus, mangetout and pinenut risotto, 113–14
aubergine sticky rice rolls, 71
fragrant basmati, 29
lemon-hazelnut risotto, 138–9
radicchio and roasted pumpkin risotto, 116
risotto, 112–16
roasted roots and couscous pilaff, 117
roast pumpkin with lemon-hazelnut risotto stuffing, 138–9
watercress and red onion risotto, 115
wild, and parsnip fritters, 96–7

risotto, 112–13
asparagus, mangetout and pinenut, 113–14
lemon-hazelnut, 138–9
radicchio and roasted pumpkin, 116
watercress and red onion, 115

roasted vegetables, 18
aubergine, 19
beetroot, 21
garlic, 106–7, 118
parsnips, 117, 138–9
peppers, 72
potatoes, spiced, 26
pumpkin, 116, 135–7
ratatouille, 90
roots, 117
squash, 27
sweet peppers, 106, 133–4
sweet potatoes, 26
tomato, 58, 104

rocket
and flat-leaf parsley salad, 48
with grilled polenta, 45
pesto, 37

roots, mixed
Moroccan-spiced vegetable and almond pastries, 122–3
roasted, and couscous pilaff, 117

rosemary
-chilli oil, 39
flageolet beans in cider and, 102–3
squash, butterbean and leek stew, 92–4
tomato and onion bread, 16–17

rosewater syrup, 163

sage and paprika butter, 69

salads, 45–55
Bridget's, 45
broad bean, spinach and beetroot, 50
rocket and flat-leaf parsley, 48
summer vegetables with mixed leaves, 47
Thai cucumber and green bean, 51
Tobias, 46
tomato, 54
tomato and fresh mozzarella, 54
tomato with rocket pesto and Knockalara sheep's cheese, 54
watercress, new potato and avocado, 52

salsas, 32–3
avocado, 33
fennel-chilli, 33
green pepper-coriander, 32

salsify and celeriac fritters, deep-fried, 83

sauces and syrups
amaretto custard, 158
blue cheese cream, 83
butterscotch, 146
coconut, with lime and coriander, 100
coconut-chilli cream, 86
coffee, 154
coffee syrup, 149
cucumber-coriander yoghurt, 122–3
gingered pumpkin cream, 116
leek and parmesan, 138–9
lemon, 120
lemon-cumin cream, 135–7
roasted garlic-chive cream, 106–7
roasted pepper, 133–4
rosewater syrup, 163
sesame-soya, 71
sweet ginger and chilli, 98
sweet-spiced beetroot cream, 70–1
tomato-coconut, 131–2
see also salsas

scallion
filling, with almond and chilli, for couscous-crusted aubergine, 126–7
soured cream and cucumber garnish, 59

sesame
-fried cabbage, 29
-soya sauce dip, 71

shortbread, rhubarb, 146

shoyu-ginger dip, 57

sorbet, dark chocolate, 162

soups, 58–60
celeriac, potato and hazelnut, 60
chilled beetroot, 58–9
roasted tomato, 58

spinach
braised parcels of feta, green pepper and caramelized onion, 70–1
broad bean and beetroot salad, 50
leek and stilton tart, 111
leeks and tomatoes with pasta ribbons in lemon sauce, 120
with chickpeas, lemon and cumin, 126–7

spring cabbage, pumpkin and almond dolma, 124

spring rolls with gingered sweet potato, 86

squash
butterbean and leek stew, 92–4
chilli-roasted, 27
see also pumpkin

starters, 43–87

stir fry of mushroom, pak choy and eggroll, 98

strawberries
little summer puddings, 150
organic, on a hazelnut pavlova, 148

summer puddings, little, 150

sundried tomato pesto, 38

sweetcorn with roast pumpkin and lemon-hazelnut risotto stuffing, 138–9

sweet potatoes
gingered spring rolls, 86
ginger-roasted, 26

tapenade
black olive, 35
dressing, 50

temperature conversion table, 12

tempura, 57

Thai dishes
cucumber and green bean salad, 51
tofu-cashew fritters, 128–9

thyme and cider, mushrooms in, 97

tiramisu terrine, iced, with coffee syrup, 149

tofu
noodles, leeks and greens, 100
Thai tofu-cashew fritters, 128–9

tomato
aubergine and mozzarella tart, 111
-coconut sauce, 131–2
coriander and puy lentil concasse, 82
crostini, 48
and fresh mozzarella salad, 54
oven-roasted, and goats' cheese and pinenut charlotte, 104
puy lentil and kale concasse, 101
roasted, soup, 58
rosemary and onion bread, 16–17
salad, 54
salad with rocket pesto and Knockalara sheep's cheese, 54
spinach and leeks with pasta ribbons in lemon sauce, 120
sundried, pesto, 38

vanilla ice cream, 163

vegetables, mixed
coconut-stewed, 128–9
summer, with mixed leaves, 47

vermicelli, crisped rice, 51

vine leaves and carrot, almond and feta terrine, 74

wafers, pistachio, 156

walnuts
baked leek and Gubbeen crêpe, 101
gingered kale and pumpkin gratin, 135–7

wasabi, 22–3
and aubergine sticky rice rolls, 71
mash, 23

watercress
new potato and avocado salad, 52
and red onion risotto, 115

wild rice and parsnip fritters, 96–7

wine, 12–13

wontons
three, in a ginger broth, 80–1

yoghurt
cucumber-coriander sauce, 122–3
orange and fennel scented, 66
pistachio and green chilli kofta, 131–2
and Spanish paprika dressing, 52